S0-BZK-904

C I T Y P A C K
R o m e

By Tim Jepson

3RD EDITION

Fodor's Travel Publications, Inc.
New York • Toronto • London • Sydney • Auckland

WWW.FODORS.COM

Contents

life 5–12

how to organize your time 13–22

top 25 sights 23–48

Index 94–95

About this book 4

best 49–60

where to... 61–86

travel facts 87–93

About this book

KEY TO SYMBOLS

🕂   map reference on the fold-out map accompanying this book (see below)

✉   address

☎   telephone number

🕓   opening times

🍴   restaurant or café on premises or nearby

🚇   nearest Metro (subway) train station

🚆   nearest overground train station

🚌   nearest bus route

🚢   nearest riverboat or ferry stop

♿   facilities for visitors with disabilities

✋   admission charge

↔   other nearby places of interest

❓   tours, lectures, or special events

➤   indicates the page where you will find a fuller description

ℹ   tourist information

Citypack Rome is divided into six sections to cover the six most important aspects of your visit to Rome. It comprises:

- The author's view of the city and its people
- Itineraries, walks, and excursions
- The top 25 sights to visit—as selected by the author
- Features on what makes the city special
- Detailed listings of restaurants, hotels, shops, and nightlife
- Practical information

In addition, easy-to-read side panels provide extra facts and snippets, highlights of places to visit, and invaluable practical advice.

CROSS-REFERENCES

To help you make the most of your visit, cross-references, indicated by ➤ , show you where to find additional information about a place or subject.

MAPS

The fold-out map in the wallet at the back of the book is a comprehensive street plan of Rome. All the map references given in the book refer to this map. For example, the Palazzo Corsini, on the Via della Lungara, has the following information: 🕂 dIV; C6—indicating the grid squares of the large-scale map (dIV) and the main map (C6) in which the Palazzo Corsini will be found.

The downtown maps found on the inside front and back covers of the book itself are for quick reference. They show the top 25 sights, described on pages 24 – 48, which are clearly plotted by number (1 – 25 , not page number) from west to east across the city.

ROME
life

INTRODUCING ROME

Rome is one of the most romantic places in the world. Soaked in the culture and history of centuries, it is the city of the Caesars, of languorous sunny days, the city of *la dolce vita*, of art, of religion, churches, and museums, of fountain-splashed piazzas and majestic monuments to its golden age of empire. In addition to these unique charms it has the temporal seductions of all Italian cities—notably superb food and wine—plus the wide-ranging attractions of a major European capital: great bars and cafés, excellent shopping, a vibrant nightlife, and numerous concerts and cultural events.

Areas of the city

Rome's ancient heart is the Roman Forum, close to Piazza Venezia (its modern center). Via del Corso strikes north to Piazza del Popolo, with the busy

Piazza della Rotonda and (left) the side of the Pantheon

shopping streets around Piazza di Spagna to its east. Corso Vittorio Emanuele II runs west to St. Peter's, bisecting the core of the medieval city (or *centro storico*). Trastevere, a quaint area of restaurants and small streets, lies across the Tiber river on its west bank. Testaccio, south of the old city, is an increasingly trendy area of bars and clubs. Prati (north of St. Peter's) and the area around Stazione Termini in the east are predominantly 19th-century creations.

To uncover the city at its most beguiling, it is worth ignoring (at least initially) the big-name sights like St. Peter's and the Colosseum, both likely to be besieged by visitors. Start instead with a stroll around the Ghetto or Trastevere, two of its quaintest old quarters, or a quiet cappuccino in one of its loveliest squares, Campo de' Fiori or Piazza Navona. Alternatively, wander into some of the city's greener corners—the Villa Borghese and Pincio Gardens. Better still, start with one of the lesser known churches, such as San Clemente, with its multilayered monuments to pagan and medieval Rome, or Santa Maria del Popolo, crammed with master-pieces by Raphael, Pinturicchio, and Caravaggio.

After this leisurely start, explore a city that mingles its magnificent past with a sometimes brash and unsettling present. Rome—more than most European capitals—is a city of extremes. The noise, bustle, and traffic in busy periods is striking. Tackle the sights without bearing this in mind, in the heat of a summer afternoon, and you will emerge the worst for wear; battered rather than enraptured. The citizens are just as startling as their city. Provincial

Italians see Romans as lazy, stubborn, slovenly, and rude. There is an old joke that if you followed the famous adage and "do as the Romans do," you would do nothing at all. As ever there is some truth in the myth. Romans excel in the art of *non mefreghismo*—not giving a damn—an infuriating habit when you want service in a bar or a little extra space on a bus. Of course there are exceptions, and in their defence Romans have had to develop thick skins to deal with a city whose facilities barely match its needs—not to mention the flood tide of tourists that further burdens its overstretched resources. This said, a smile and a little stuttered Italian usually brings courtesy, and after a while the Roman gruffness can become almost endearing. You will begin to enjoy the city's Fellini-esque cast of characters: pot-bellied restaurateurs, dog-walking old women, fallen aristocrats, grumpy bar-tenders, and rough-fingered matriarchs of the market stalls.

Vatican City

Vatican City is the world's smallest independent sovereign state (just over 100 acres). Its 200 inhabitants (about 30 of whom are women) are presided over by the Pope, Europe's only absolute monarch. Around 800 "foreigners" commute in and out to work, but the general public is admitted only to areas like St. Peter's and the Vatican Museums. The city has its own civil service and judicial systems, shops, banks, currency, stamps, post office, garages—even its own helicopter pad, radio station, and newspaper (*L'Osservatore Romano*). Its official language is still Latin.

One of the matriarchs of the Roman market stands

ROME IN FIGURES

History
- Official age of the city (in 2000): 2,753 years
- Number of popes: 168
- Number of emperors: 73
- Number of vestal virgins at any one time: 6
- Length of service of a vestal virgin: 30 years
- Water delivered by aqueducts to Rome in the 2nd century AD: 312,000 gallons
- Number of obelisks: 20 (of which Egyptian: 7)

Geography
- Fabled number of hills: 7 (Palatine, Celian, Capitoline, Aventine, Quirinal, Esquiline, Viminal)
- Actual number of hills: 20
- Distance from the sea: 17 miles
- Area of the city: 577 square miles
- Total length of Metro: 15.4 miles
- Length of Vatican–Rome railroad: 2,828 feet

People
- Official population: 2,777,882
- Unofficial population: 4.5 million
- Estimated tourists annually: 15 million
- Size of average family: 2.7
- People living in illegally built homes: 700,000

Religion
- Number of churches within the city walls: 280
- Romans who have had their children baptized: 94 percent
- Romans who favor women priests: 40 percent
- Romans who do not condemn divorce: 80 percent
- Romans who believe in hell: 40 percent
- Romans who never go to confession: 60 percent
- Romans who sometimes go to mass: 23 percent
- Romans who go to both mass and confession weekly: 12 percent
- Romans who profess themselves Catholics, but who do not follow the Church's "moral teaching": 78 percent
- Romans who believe they have been affected by the "evil eye": 37 percent

ROME PEOPLE

THE POPE

Rome's first bishop was St. Peter. Since then his successors have been considered Christ's representatives on earth and continue to hold sway over the world's Roman Catholics (who today number some 850 million). For centuries popes also ruled large areas of Italy (they only relinquished control of Rome in 1870). Papal election—conducted by a conclave of cardinals in the Sistine Chapel—is achieved by one of three methods: acclamation, in which divine intervention causes all present to call one name in unison (not common); by majority vote, with votes cast four times daily until a candidate has a two-thirds majority; and by compromise, on the recommendation of a commission.

VALENTINO

The doyen of Rome's fashion designers has no rivals in his home city. Having risen to prominence in the heady dolce vita days of the late 1950s, Valentino quickly established a name for exquisite (and exquisitely expensive) haute couture, dressing many stars of stage, screen, and high society. More recently, he has diversified into ready-to-wear. To visit his palatial showrooms around Piazza di Spagna, however, is to realize that the master's touch is still appreciated and bought.

John Paul II was the first Polish pope

Devil's Advocate

The Vatican still has an office for the Avvocato del Diavolo —the Devil's Advocate—from which the expression derives. His job is to investigate the lives of prospective saints and those put forward for beatification to discover why they might not be acceptable.

The President

Rome is Italy's political capital, and as well as being home to the country's lower and upper chambers (housed in Palazzo Montecitorio, the Chamber of Deputies—and Palazzo Madama—the Senate) it is also home to her head of state, the President (whose offices are in the Palazzo del Quirinale). The post is largely symbolic.

A Chronology

1200–800 BC	First settlements on the banks of the Tiber.
753 BC	Traditional date of the foundation of Rome by Romulus, first of the city's seven kings.
616–578 BC	Tarquinius Priscus, Rome's first Etruscan king.
509 BC	Etruscans expelled and the Republic founded.
390 BC	Rome briefly occupied by the Gauls.
264–241 BC	First Punic War against Carthage (North Africa).
218–201 BC	Second Punic War: Rome threatened by Hannibal, leader of the Carthaginian army.
149–146 BC	Third Punic War: Rome defeats Carthage.
60 BC	Rome ruled by a triumvirate of Pompey, Marcus Licinius Crassus, and Julius Caesar.
48 BC	Caesar declared ruler for life but assassinated by jealous rivals in 44 BC.
27 BC–AD 14	Rule of Octavian, Caesar's great-nephew, who as Augustus becomes the first Roman emperor.
AD 42	St. Peter the Apostle visits Rome.
54–68	Reign of Nero. Great Fire in AD 64; "Nero fiddles while Rome burns." Christian persecutions.
72	The Colosseum is begun.
98–117	Reign of Emperor Trajan. Military campaigns greatly extend the Empire's boundaries.
117–38	Reign of Emperor Hadrian.
161–180	Reign of Emperor Marcus Aurelius, general and philosopher. Barbarians attack Empire's borders.
284–286	Empire divided into East and West.
306–337	The Emperor Constantine reunites the Empire and legalizes Christianity. St. Peter's and the first Christian churches are built.

410	Rome is sacked by the Goths.
476	Romulus Augustulus is the last Roman emperor.
800	Charlemagne awards some territories to papacy; Pope Leo III crowns him Holy Roman Emperor.
1378–1417	The Great Schism between rival papal claimants. Papacy to Avignon, France.
1452–1626	The new St. Peter's is built.
1483	Birth of Raphael.
1508	Michelangelo begins the Sistine Chapel ceiling.
1527	Rome is sacked and looted by German and Spanish troops under Charles V.
1598	Birth of baroque sculptor and architect Gian Lorenzo Bernini.
1732–1735	Fontana di Trevi and Spanish Steps begun.
1797	Napoleon occupies Rome until 1814, when power is restored to the Papal States.
1848	Uprisings in Rome under Mazzini and Garibaldi force Pope Pius IX to flee. The new "Roman Republic" is ultimately defeated by the French.
1870	Rome joins a united Italy.
1922	Fascists march on Rome; Mussolini becomes Prime Minister. Fascists rule Italy 1924–43.
1929	The Lateran Treaty recognizes the Vatican as a separate state.
1940	Italy enters World War II with the Axis powers (Allies liberate Rome from Nazis in 1944).
1960	Rome hosts the Olympic games.
1978	Karol Wojtyla is elected Pope John Paul II.
1990	Soccer's World Cup Final held in Rome.

PEOPLE & EVENTS FROM HISTORY

Capitoline Wolf, *suckling Romulus and Remus, Palazzo dei Conservatori* (► 37)

ROMULUS AND REMUS

The myth of Rome's birth was recorded by Livy (Titus Livius, 59 BC–AD 17), and begins in the old Latin capital Alba Longa with the king Numitor, whose throne was stolen by his brother Amulius. To prevent rival claims Amulius forced Numitor's daughter, Rhea, to become a vestal virgin. The god Mars then appeared to Rhea and left her pregnant with Romulus and Remus. The twins, when born, were cast adrift by Amulius, but were guided by the gods to the Velabrum, the old marshes under the Palatine Hill. Here they were suckled by a she-wolf and eventually adopted by a shepherd. In adulthood, fulfilling a prophecy made by Mars, they founded Rome in 753 BC. Both wished to rule, but neither could agree on a name for the new city. Remus favored Rema, while Romulus preferred Roma. Romulus settled the argument by murdering his brother and built the city walls.

The Sack of Rome

One of the single most traumatic events in Rome's long history took place in 1527, when the city was sacked by German and Spanish troops from the imperial army of Charles V. Countless buildings and works of art were destroyed while Pope Clement VII took refuge in the Castel Sant'Angelo. Over 4,000 people died in the siege. The plunder of the city then went on for several weeks.

JULIUS CAESAR

Caesar originally intended to become a priest, joining the army in 81 BC to pay his debts. He eventually became Pontifex Maximus, Rome's high priest, and then joined Pompey and Crassus in 60 BC in ruling Rome as the "First Triumvirate." Over the next ten years he fought military campaigns in Gaul and Germany, and launched two short invasions of Britain. His successes aroused the envy of Pompey, who eventually fled Rome at the news that Caesar had crossed the Rubicon with his returning army. For six months Caesar pursued Pompey across Spain, Greece, and Africa, and also spent time with Cleopatra. In 48 BC he was appointed Rome's absolute ruler. He was assassinated in 44 BC on March 15 (the "Ides of March"), murdered by a group of envious conspirators that included Brutus, his adopted son.

ROME
how to organize your time

ITINERARIES

During a short visit it is only possible to skim the surface of this great city's cultural and artistic heritage. The best course is to concentrate on a few sights in a single area (but do take opening times into account).

ITINERARY ONE	ANCIENT ROME
Breakfast	Latteria del Gallo (➤ 68) or an outdoor café in Campo de' Fiori (➤ 29).
Morning	Stroll through the Ghetto district (➤ 18) to Piazza del Campidoglio. Santa Maria in Aracoeli (➤ 38) and Capitoline Museums (➤ 37). Roman Forum and the Palatine (➤ 41). Colosseum (➤ 43). Arch of Constantine (➤ 50).
Lunch	Picnic in the Parco Oppio park (➤ 56), snack in Enoteca, Via Cavour 313, or lunch in Da Valentino (➤ 64) or Nerone (➤ 63).
Afternoon	San Pietro in Vincoli (➤ 44). San Clemente (➤ 46). San Giovanni in Laterano (➤ 48). Metro to Termini then Santa Maria Maggiore (➤ 47).

ITINERARY TWO	PANTHEON TO ST. PETER'S
Breakfast	Piazza della Rotonda or a bar nearby: La Tazza d'Oro, Sant'Eustachio or Camilloni (➤ 69).
Morning	Santa Maria sopra Minerva (➤ 34). Pantheon (➤ 33). San Luigi dei Francesi (➤ 30). Piazza Navona (➤ 30). Coffee at Bar della Pace (➤ 68). Via dei Coronari or Via del Governo Vecchio. Castel Sant'Angelo (➤ 27).
Lunch	Picnic in the Parco Adriano.
Afternoon	St. Peter's (➤ 24), then Vatican Museums (➤ 25) and Sistine Chapel (➤ 26).
Evening	Dine and stroll in Trastevere (➤ 18).

ITINERARY THREE	**THE CORSO TO THE VATICAN**
	Via del Corso and Column of Marcus Aurelius (➤ 51), then Fontana di Trevi (➤ 39).
Breakfast	Bar by the Fontana di Trevi (➤ 39).
Morning	Walk up Via delle Scuderie and Via Rasella to the Palazzo Barberini (➤ 42). Piazza di Spagna and Spanish Steps (➤ 40), Museo Keats–Shelley (➤ 40, 52). Coffee at Caffè Greco or Babington's Tea Rooms (➤ 69). Pincio Gardens (➤ 57). Santa Maria del Popolo (➤ 32).
Lunch	Picnic in the Pincio Gardens or Villa Borghese (both ➤ 57); or snack at the Rosati or Canova bars (➤ 68).
Afternoon	Ara Parcis Augustae (➤ 31). Walk to Piazza del Risorgimento or take bus 49 from Piazza Cavour. Vatican Museums (➤ 25), Sistine Chapel (➤ 26).
Evening	Stroll and dine near Piazza di Spagna (➤ 40).
ITINERARY FOUR	**TOWARDS TRASTEVERE**
Breakfast	Antico Caffè Brasile (➤ 69).
Morning	Trajan's Markets (➤ 51). Palazzo-Galleria Colonna (➤ 53). Palazzo-Galleria Doria Pamphili (➤ 36). Piazza Venezia: Santa Maria in Aracoeli (➤ 38) and Capitoline Museums (➤ 37).
Lunch	Light lunch in Birreria Fratelli Tempera (➤ 64).
Afternoon	Walk to Santa Maria in Cosmedin (➤ 60) via Piazza del Campidoglio and Piazza della Consolazione, then Circus Maximus (➤ 51). Isola Tiberina. Santa Cecilia in Trastevere (➤ 16) and Santa Maria in Trastevere (➤ 28). Coffee at Trastè (➤ 68).

WALKS

Temple of Vesta

THE SIGHTS

- Santa Maria in Aracoeli
  (➤ 38)
- Capitoline Museums
  (➤ 37)
- Santa Maria in Cosmedin
  (➤ 60)
- Temple of Vesta
- Teatro di Marcello: medieval
  houses over Roman theater
- San Bartolomeo: 11th
  century, over pagan temple
- Santa Cecilia in Trastevere:
  altar canopy, mosaic, frescoes
- Santa Maria in Trastevere
  (➤ 28)
- Villa Farnesina (➤ 53)
- Palazzo Spada (➤ 53)
- Chiesa Nuova or Santa
  Maria in Vallicella: frescoes,
  Oratorio and clock tower
- Castel Sant'Angelo (➤ 27)
- St. Peter's (➤ 24)

INFORMATION

Time 2–4 hours
Distance 3 miles
Start point Piazza Venezia
End point St. Peter's
🕐 See Capitoline Museums and
   churches first (most close
   noon). The Castel Sant'
   Angelo may be shut when
   you arrive. St. Peter's closes
   7PM (summer), 6PM (winter)
🍴 Trastè (➤ 68)

FROM PIAZZA VENEZIA TO ST. PETER'S THROUGH THE HISTORIC CITY CENTER AND TRASTEVERE

Start at Piazza Venezia. Take Via del Teatro di Marcello to the steps of Piazza del Campidoglio. At the south corner of the piazza, Via del Campidoglio leads to a view over the Forum, then to Via della Consolazione and Santa Maria in Cosmedin. From Piazza della Consolazione walk south to Piazza Bocca della Verità. Follow Lungotevere dei Pierleoni north along the river, and cross Ponte Fabricio to Isola Tiberina.

Cross Ponte Cestio and follow Via Anicia south to Santa Cecilia in Trastevere. Cut northwest to Viale di Trastevere and Piazza Sidney Sonnino, and follow Via della Lungaretta west to Piazza Santa Maria in Trastevere. Leave the piazza to the north, towards Vicolo dei Cinque and Piazza Trilussa. If you have time, walk west to Via della Lungara to see the Villa Farnesina. Cross the Ponte Sisto, follow Via dei Pettinari northeast, and turn northwest on Via Capo di Ferro to Piazza Farnese and Campo de' Fiori. (Detour southwest from Piazza Farnese to Via dei Farnesi to look at elegant Via Giulia and Santa Maria dell'Orazione e Morte ➤ 29.) Take Via dei Cappellari northwest from Campo de' Fiori, turn left on Via del Pellegrino and then right on Via dei Cartari to reach Corso Vittorio Emanuele II. Pick up Via dei Filippini to the west of Chiesa Nuova. Turn left on Via dei Banchi Nuovi and then right on Via Banco di Santo Spirito. Cross the Ponte Sant'Angelo. Follow Via della Conciliazione west to St. Peter's.

A CIRCULAR WALK FROM PIAZZA NAVONA THROUGH THE HEART OF THE MEDIEVAL CITY

Begin in Piazza Navona. Leave via the alley in the southeast corner, cross Corso del Rinascimento and follow Via degli Staderari past Sant'Ivo (inside the Palazzo di Sapienza) and Sant'Eustachio. Take Via Santa Chiara east to Piazza della Minerva and then Via Minerva north to Piazza della Rotonda.

Take Via del Seminario east from the Piazza then turn right on Via Sant'Ignazio and into Piazza Collegio Romano. Cross Via del Corso to the east and wind northeast through Via Santi Apostoli, Via San Marcello, and Via dell'Umiltà to emerge just south of the Fontana di Trevi. Follow Via del Lavatore, Via delle Scuderie, and Via Rasella east to Palazzo Barberini. Walk north to Piazza Barberini; detour briefly north up Via Vittorio Veneto to see Santa Maria della Concezione in the Convento dei Cappuccini, then head northwest on Via Sistina to explore the Spanish Steps (Piazza di Spagna) and the chic shopping streets nearby. Climb back up the steps and take Viale Trinità dei Monti to the Pincio Gardens and Villa Borghese.

Drop down west to Piazza del Popolo and walk south along Via di Ripetta to the Altar of Peace and the Mausoleum of Augustus. From Piazza Porta di Ripetta follow Via Borghese and Via Divino Amore south to little Piazza Firenze. Continue south to Piazza della Rotonda

Piazza del Popolo

by way of Piazza in Campo Marzio and Via Maddalena. Take Via Giustiniani west to San Luigi, then follow Via della Scrofa north to Sant'Agostino before returning to Piazza Navona.

THE SIGHTS

- Sant'Ivo alla Sapienza
- Santa Maria sopra Minerva (➤ 34)
- Pantheon (➤ 33)
- Palazzo-Galleria Doria Pamphili (➤ 36)
- Fontana di Trevi (➤ 39)
- Palazzo Barberini (➤ 42)
- Santa Maria della Concezione (➤ 60)
- Spanish Steps (➤ 40)
- Pincio Gardens (➤ 57)
- Villa Borghese (➤ 57)
- Santa Maria del Popolo (➤ 32)
- Altar of Peace (➤ 31)
- Palazzo Borghese
- San Luigi dei Francesi (➤ 30)
- Sant'Agostino: Caravaggio's *Madonna*, Raphael's *Isaiah*

INFORMATION

Time 4–6 hours
Distance 3½ miles (circular tour)
Start/end point Piazza Navona
🚇 eI; C5
🚌 46, 62, 64 to Corso Vittorio Emanuele II, or 70, 81, 87, 492, 628, 186 to Corso del Rinascimento
🕐 Start early with Palazzo-Galleria Doria Pamphili and Palazzo Barberini. Churches at the end of the walk are open late afternoon
🍴 Bar della Pace, Doney, Rosati and Canova (➤ 68). For ice cream: Tre Scalini, and the Gelateria della Palma (➤ 67)

17

EVENING STROLLS

INFORMATION

Ghetto
Start point Via Arenula
➕ eIII–fIV; C6–D6
🚌 44, 46, 56, 60, 61, 64, 65, 70, 75, 81, 87 to Largo di Torre Argentina; or 8, 44, 46, 56, 60, 61, 64, 65, 70, 75, 170, 181 to Via Arenula; or all services to Piazza Venezia
🕓 The empty, echoing streets of the Ghetto are best seen late at night

Trastevere
Start point Piazza Sidney Sonnino
➕ eIV; C6
🚌 8, 44, 56, 60, 75, 170, 181 to Piazza Sidney Sonnino

18   *Fontana delle Tartarughe*

THE GHETTO
The old Jewish Ghetto occupies the quaint quadrangle of streets and alleys formed by Via delle Botteghe Oscure, Via Arenula, Lungotevere dei Cenci, and Via del Teatro di Marcello. Many descendants of the Jews who were first forced to move here in 1556 still live and work in the district (there is a synagogue overlooking the Tiber at Lungotevere dei Cenci). Any combination of routes through the area offers intriguing little corners, though the one sight you should be sure not to miss is the charming Fontana delle Tartarughe in Piazza Mattei. This can be seen by walking down Via dei Falegnami from Via Arenula. Thereafter you might wander south on Via Sant'Ambrogio to Via Portico d'Ottavia, where you can see the remains of a 2nd-century BC gateway and colonnade. Striking north from here to Piazza Campitelli and Piazza Margana will also reveal some enchanting nooks and crannies. At night the area is almost deserted, but it is well lit and should be perfectly safe.

TRASTEVERE
Almost every city has an area like Trastevere, a district whose tightly-knit streets and intrinsic charm single it out as a focus for eating and nightlife. Trastevere (derived from the Latin *Trans Tiberim*—literally "across the Tiber") was once the heart of Rome's 19th-century working-class suburbs, and parts of its fringes are still slightly rough and ready (and so worth avoiding in the dead of night). A good way to discover the area is to take the Via della Lungaretta from Piazza Sidney Sonnino to Piazza di Santa Maria in Trastevere and then explore some of the smaller streets to the north, such as Vicolo dei Cinque and Via del Moro. At night be sure to take in the floodlit facade of Santa Maria in Trastevere (► 28). To see the churches, especially Santa Cecilia (► 16), time your stroll for early morning or late afternoon. You'll also need to return during the day to visit the Villa Farnesina (► 53), the botanical gardens (► 56), and the market in Piazza San Cosimato (► 77).

ORGANIZED SIGHTSEEING

AMERICAN EXPRESS
American Express runs bus tours around Rome,
Tivoli, and farther afield to Pompeii, Naples, and
Capri. The Tivoli tour (➤ 21) includes Hadrian's
Villa and the Villa d'Este. The company also
organizes three- to four-hour walks of the city
with English-speaking guides: the Vatican City
tour, which takes in the Vatican Museums
(➤ 25), Sistine Chapel (➤ 26), and St. Peter's
(➤ 24); "Rome of the Caesars"; and "Religious
Rome," which visits the Catacombs, Pantheon
(➤ 33), Piazza Navona (➤ 30), and St. Peter's.
Reservations are advisable at busy times.

✚ D5 ✉ Piazza di Spagna 38 ☎ 06 67641 🕐 Apr–Sep: Mon–Fri
9–5:30; Sat 9–3. Oct–Mar: Mon–Fri 9–5:30; Sat 9–12:30 🚇 Spagna
🚌 119 to Piazza di Spagna

APPIAN LINE
Many travel agents organize guided tours (try
those in Piazza della Repubblica). Appian Line,
close to Santa Maria Maggiore, is one of the best
known. The tours of the city and destinations
farther out are a little cheaper than those of
American Express. Reservations are unneces-
sary for local itineraries: simply turn up at the
office 15 minutes before your tour departs.

✚ E5 ✉ Piazza Esquilino 6 ☎ 06 487861 🕐 Daily 7:30AM–
8:30PM 🚇 Termini 🚌 4, 9, 14, 16, 27 to Piazza Esquilino

GREEN LINE TOURS
Green Line operates trips similar to those organ-
ized by American Express and Appian Line at
prices about midway between the two. No
reservations necessary.

✚ E5 ✉ Via Farini 5a ☎ 06 482 7480 🕐 Daily 7AM–8:30PM
🚇 Termini 🚌 4, 9, 14, 16, 27 to Piazza Esquilino

OTHER OPTIONS
Other reputable guided bus and walking tour
firms include **CIT** (✉ Piazza della Repubblica 64 ☎ 06
47941) and **Carrani Tours** (✉ Via Vittorio Emanuele Orlando 95
☎ 06 474 2501). CIT, Appian, and Carrani all organize trips to the Pope's Sunday blessing at Castel
Gandolfo in the Appian Hills. Carrani will also
organize papal audiences and (like Appian) a tour
of Rome at night with accordionists.

*The Tiber and two
of its bridges*

Inexpensive tours
One of the cheapest and most
relaxed tours of Rome can be
enjoyed, albeit without
commentary, by boarding
streetcar 19 or 30, both of which
meander through some of the
most interesting parts of the city.
Or take the official public
transportation (ATAC) tour: with
five departures daily (at 10:30, 2,
3, 5, and 6) the 110 bus makes a
two-hour circuit from Piazza dei
Cinquecento (with five stops en
route). A brief multilingual
commentary and a free
multilingual brochure are included
with tickets, available from the
ATAC kiosk on concourse C in
Piazza dei Cinquecento (☎ 06
4695 2252/2256) from 3PM.

EXCURSIONS

Ostia Antica

FRASCATI

Frascati, cradled in the Alban Hills, makes the easiest and most accessible day (or half-day) trip from Rome. Famous for its white wine, it is also known for its broad views and cooling summer breezes. Small trains ply the branch line to the town, rattling though vineyards and olive groves beyond the city's sprawling suburbs. There is little to do—most pleasure is to be had wandering the streets—but you should see the gardens of the Villa Aldobrandini (above the main Piazza Marconi) and sample a refreshing glass of Frascati in one of the town's many wine cellars.

OSTIA ANTICA

Untrumpeted Ostia Antica, 15 miles southwest of Rome, is Italy's best-preserved Roman town after Pompeii and Herculaneum, its extensive ruins and lovely rural site as appealing as any in Rome itself. Built at the mouth (*ostium*) of the Tiber as ancient Rome's seaport, it became a vast and bustling colony before silt and the Empire's decline together hastened its demise. Among the many excavated buildings are countless *horrea*, or warehouses, and several multi-story apartment blocks known as *insulae*. Other highlights at the site include the Piazzale delle Corporazioni, the heart of the old business district; the 4,000-seat amphitheater; and the small Ostiense Museum.

TIVOLI

Tivoli is by far the most popular excursion from Rome, thanks to the town's lovely wooded position, the superlative gardens of the Villa d'Este, and the ruins and grounds of Hadrian's vast Roman villa (4 miles southwest). The Este gardens were laid out in 1550 as part of a country retreat for Cardinal Ippolito d'Este, son of Lucrezia Borgia and the Duke of Ferrara. The highlights among the beautifully integrated terraces and many fountains are Gian Lorenzo Bernini's elegant Fontana di Bicchierone and the vast Viale delle Cento Fontane ("Avenue of the Hundred Fountains"). Hadrian's Villa, the largest ever conceived in the Roman world, was built between AD 118 and 135 and covered an area as great as the center of imperial Rome.

Villa d'Este gardens, Tivoli

TARQUINIA

This site is bound to interest you in the story of the Etruscans. Tarquinia, northwest of Rome, was one of three major Etruscan cities—the others are present-day Vulci and Cerveteri—and was the cultural, artistic, and probably political capital of the civilization. Founded in the 10th century BC, its population once touched 100,000, declining from the 4th century BC with the rise of Rome. The town's Museo Nazionale houses a fascinating assortment of Etruscan art and artifacts, including the famous winged horses, though it is the number of nearby Etruscan tombs, the Necropoli (many beautifully painted), that draw most visitors (1–3 miles from town).

INFORMATION

Tivoli
Distance 19 miles
Journey time 40 minutes
Villa d'Este
- ✉ Piazza Trento ☎ 0774 312070 🕐 Summer: Tue–Sun 9–7. Winter: Tue–Sun 9–5 💰 Expensive
Villa Adriana
- ✉ Via Tiburtina ☎ 0774 530203 🕐 May–Aug: daily 9–6:30. Mar and Sep: daily 9–5:30. Nov–Jan: daily 9–4. Feb and Oct: daily 9–5. Apr: 9–6 💰 Expensive
- 🍴 Sibilla, Via della Sibilla 50. Refreshments also at Villa d'Este and Villa Adriana
- 🚉 Train to Tivoli from Termini, then 30-minute walk or local bus No. 4
- 🚌 COTRAL bus from Via Gaeta or Metro line B to Rebibbia, and COTRAL bus to Tivoli

Tarquinia
Distance 60 miles
Journey time 70 minutes
Museo Nazionale
- ✉ Palazzo Vitelleschi
- 🕐 Museum Tue–Sun 9–7. Necropoli Apr–Sep: Tue–Sun 9–7. Oct–Mar: Tue–Sun 9–5
- 🚌 Metro line A to Lepanto, then COTRAL bus from corner of Viale Giulio Cesare and Via Lepanto
- 🚉 Train to Tarquinia from Termini, then shuttle bus
- 💰 Expensive (see Museo Nazionale ticket office for museum and tombs ☎ 0766 856036)
- ℹ Piazza Cavour 1 ☎ 0766 856384

WHAT'S ON

January	*La Befana* (Jan 6): Epiphany celebrations; fair and market in Piazza Navona.
February	*Carnevale* (week before Lent): Costume festivities on the streets; parties on Shrove Tuesday.
March	*Festa di San Giuseppe* (Mar 19): Street stalls in the Trionfale area north of the Vatican.
	Festa della Primavera (late Mar–Apr): Thousands of azaleas arranged on the Spanish Steps.
April	*Good Friday* (Mar/Apr): Procession of the Cross at 9PM to the Colosseum, led by the Pope.
	Easter Sunday (Mar/Apr): Pope addresses the crowds at noon in Piazza di San Pietro.
	Rome's Birthday (Apr 21): Flags and pageantry on Piazza del Campidoglio.
May	*International Horse Show* (early May): Concorso Ippico in Villa Borghese.
June	*Feste della Repubblica* (Jun 2): Military parade along Via dei Fori Imperiali.
	Festa di San Giovanni (Jun 23–24): Fair, food, and fireworks around San Giovanni in Laterano.
July	*Tevere Expo* (last week Jun/Jul): Food and handicrafts fair on the banks of the Tiber between the Cavour and Sant'Angelo bridges.
	Festa dei Noiantri (week beginning third Sunday in July): Street fairs and processions in Trastevere.
	Jazz Festival di Roma (end of Jun/Jul).
August	*Ferragosto* (Aug 15): Feast of the Assumption; everything closes.
September	*Art Fair*: Via Margutta.
	Sagra dell'Uva (early Sep): Wine and harvest festival in the Basilica di Massenzio.
October	*Antiques Fair* (mid-Oct) Via dei Coronari.
November	*Ognissanti* (Nov 1–2): All Saints' Day.
	Festa di Santa Cecilia (Nov 22) in the catacombs and church of Santa Cecilia in Trastevere.
December	*Festa della Madonna Immacolata* (Dec 8): Pope and other dignitaries leave flowers at the statue of the Madonna in Piazza di Spagna.
	Nativity Scenes (mid-Dec to mid-Jan): Crèches (*presepi*) in many Rome churches.
	Christmas Eve: Midnight Mass in many churches. Two of the most striking are in Santa Maria Maggiore and Santa Maria in Aracoeli.
	Christmas Day: Papal address and blessing in Piazza San Pietro.
	New Year's Eve: Firework displays.

ROME's
top 25 sights

These sights are shown on the maps on the inside front cover and inside back cover, numbered **1–25** *from west to east across the city*

1

BASILICA DI SAN PIETRO

HIGHLIGHTS

- Facade
- Dome
- *Pietà*, Michelangelo
- *Baldacchino*, Bernini
- *St. Peter*, Arnolfo di Cambio
- Tomb of Paul III, Guglielmo della Porta
- Tomb of Urban VIII, Bernini
- Monument to Alexander VII, Bernini
- Monument to the Last Stuarts, Canova
- View from the dome

INFORMATION

- bIII; B5
- Piazza San Pietro, Vatican City
- 06 698 4466/4866
- Basilica mid-Mar to Oct: daily 7–7. Nov to mid-Mar: daily 7–6. Dome mid-Mar to Oct: daily 8–6. Nov to mid-Mar: daily 8–4. Grottoes Apr–Sep: daily 7–6. Oct–Mar: daily 7–5. Treasury Apr–Sep: daily 9–6:30. Oct–Mar: daily 9–5:30
- Shop
- Ottaviano
- 64 to Piazza San Pietro, or 19, 23, 49, 81, 492, 991 to Piazza del Risorgimento
- Wheelchair access
- Basilica free. Dome and Treasury moderate. Grottoes expensive
- Vatican Museums (➤ 25), Sistine Chapel (➤ 26), Castel Sant'Angelo (➤ 27)

Although the works of art in St. Peter's are rather disappointing—a Michelangelo sculpture aside—the interior still manages to impress as the spiritual capital of Roman Catholicism with an overwhelming sense of scale and decorative splendor.

History The first St. Peter's was built by Constantine around AD 326, reputedly on the site where St. Peter was buried following his crucifixion in AD 64. Much later, between 1506 and 1626, it was virtually rebuilt to plans by Bramante, and then to designs by Antonio da Sangallo, Giacomo della Porta,

Baldacchino *and dome*

Michelangelo, and Carlo Maderno. Michelangelo was also responsible for much of the dome, and Bernini finished the facade and the interior.

What to see Michelangelo's unforgettable *Pietà* (1499), behind glass following an attack in 1972, is in the first chapel of the right nave. At the end of the same nave stands a statue of St. Peter: his right foot has been caressed by millions since 1857 when Pius IX granted a 50-day indulgence to anyone kissing it after confession. Bernini's high altar canopy, or *baldacchino* (1624–33), was built during the papacy of Urban VIII, a scion of the Barberini family; it is decorated with bees, the Barberinis' dynastic symbol. To its rear are Guglielmo della Porta's Tomb of Paul III (left) and Bernini's influential Tomb of Urban VIII (right). Rome seen from the dome (entrance at the end of the right nave) is *the* highlight of a visit.

MUSEI VATICANI

The Vatican Museums make up the world's largest museum complex. The 1,400 rooms abound in riches: Greek, Roman, and Etruscan sculptures, Renaissance paintings, books, maps and tapestries, and frescoes in the Raphael Rooms and the Sistine Chapel.

Treasures of 12 museums Instead of the two days (and 4 miles of walking) needed to do justice to the Vatican Museums, you can follow one of the color-coded walks, designed to ease your way through the crowds and match the time you have available. Or you might decide on your own priorities, choosing between the collections according to your interest: Egyptian and Assyrian art (the Museo Gregoriano Egizio); Etruscan artifacts (Museo Gregoriano-Etrusco); the more esoteric anthropological collections (Museo Missionario Etnologico); or modern religious art (Collezione d'Arte Religiosa Moderna).

Celebrated works of art Whatever your priorities, several sights should not be missed. Most obvious are the Sistine Chapel (➤ 26), with Michelangelo's *Last Judgment*, and the four rooms of the Stanze di Raffaello, each of which is decorated with frescoes by Raphael. Further fresco cycles by Pinturicchio and Fra Angelico adorn the Borgia Apartment and Chapel of Nicholas V, and are complemented by an almost unmatched collection of paintings in the Vatican Art Gallery (or Pinacoteca). The best of the Greek and Roman sculpture is the breathtaking Laocoön group in the Cortile Ottagono of the Museo Pio-Clementino. The list of artists whose work is shown in the Collezione di Arte Religiosa Moderna is a roll call of the most famous in the last 100 years, from Paul Gauguin and Pablo Picasso to Salvador Dalí and Henry Moore.

HIGHLIGHTS

- Sistine Chapel (➤ 26)
- Laocoön
- Apollo del Belvedere (Museo Pio-Clementino)
- *Marte di Todi* (Museo Gregoriano-Etrusco)
- Maps Gallery (Galleria delle Carte Geografiche)
- Frescoes by Pinturicchio
- Frescoes by Fra Angelico
- Stanze di Raffaello
- Pinacoteca
- Room of the Animals (Museo Pio-Clementino)

INFORMATION

- ✚ b1; B5
- ✉ Viale Vaticano, Città del Vaticano
- ☎ 06 6988 4947/4466/3333
- 🕐 Mid-Mar to Oct: Mon–Fri 8:45–4:45; Sat and last Sun of month 8:45–1:45. Nov to mid-Mar: Mon–Sat and last Sun of month 8:45–1:45. Closed public hols
- 🍴 Café, restaurant, and shop
- Ⓜ Ottaviano
- 🚌 19, 23, 81, 492 to Piazza del Risorgimento, or 64 to Piazza San Pietro
- ♿ Wheelchair-accessible routes
- 💰 Very expensive (includes entry to all other Vatican museums); free last Sun of month
- ↔ St. Peter's (➤ 24), Sistine Chapel (➤ 26), Castel Sant'Angelo (➤ 27)

25

CAPPELLA SISTINA

HIGHLIGHTS

- Ceiling frescoes, Michelangelo
- Last Judgment, Michelangelo
- Baptism of Christ in the Jordan, Perugino
- Fresco: Temptation of Christ, Botticelli
- Calling of SS Peter and Andrew, Ghirlandaio
- The Delivery of the Keys to St. Peter, Perugino
- Fresco: Moses's Journey into Egypt, Pinturicchio
- Moses Kills the Egyptian, Botticelli
- Last Days of Moses, Luca Signorelli

INFORMATION

- ✚ bI; B5
- ✉ Viale Vaticano, Città del Vaticano
- ☎ 06 6988 4947/4466/3333
- ◷ Mid-Mar to Oct: Mon–Fri 8:45–4:45; Sat and last Sun of month 8:45–1:45. Nov to mid-Mar: Mon–Sat and last Sun of month 8:45–1:45. Closed public hols
- 🍴 Café, restaurant, and shop
- Ⓜ Ottaviano
- 🚌 19, 23, 81, 492 to Piazza del Risorgimento, or 64 to Piazza San Pietro
- ♿ Wheelchair-accessible routes
- 💶 Very expensive (includes entry to all other Vatican museums)
- ↔ St. Peter's (➤ 24), Vatican Museums (➤ 25), Castel Sant'Angelo (➤ 27)

In Michelangelo's frescoes the Sistine Chapel has one of the world's supreme masterpieces. Controversially restored between 1980 and 1994, the paintings of this modest-sized, hall-like chapel at the heart of the Vatican Museums draw a ceaseless stream of pilgrims.

The chapel The Cappella Sistina (Sistine Chapel) was built by Pope Sixtus IV between 1475 and 1480. The Vatican Palace's principal chapel, it is used by the conclave of cardinals when they assemble to elect a new pope. Decoration of its lower side walls took place between 1481 and 1483, the work, among others, of Perugino, Botticelli, Ghirlandaio, Pinturicchio, and Luca Signorelli. From the chapel entrance their 12 paintings compose *Scenes from the Life of Christ* (on the left wall as you face away from the high altar) and *Scenes from the Life of Moses* (on the right wall).

Michelangelo's frescoes Michelangelo was commissioned by Pope Julius II to paint the ceiling in 1508. The frescoes, comprising over 300 individual figures, were completed in four years, most of which Michelangelo spent in appalling conditions, lying on his back and in extremes of heat and cold. Their narrative describes in nine scenes the story of Genesis and the history of humanity before the coming of Christ. In the center is the *Creation of Adam*. The fresco behind the high altar, the *Last Judgment*, was begun for Pope Paul III in 1534 and completed in 1541. An extraordinary work of art, it is densely crowded with figures, conveying a powerful sense of movement. It also shows Michelangelo in a more somber mood, with the righteous rising to paradise accompanied by angels on Christ's right, and the damned drawn irrevocably toward hell on his left.

CASTEL SANT'ANGELO

Castel Sant'Angelo, rising above the river, has served as an army barracks, papal citadel, imperial tomb, and medieval prison. Today a 58-room museum here traces the castle's near 2,000-year history, providing a pleasant contrast to the Vatican Museums.

Many incarnations The Castel Sant'Angelo was built by the Emperor Hadrian in AD 130 as a mausoleum for himself, his family, and his dynastic successors. It was crowned by a gilded chariot driven by a statue of Hadrian disguised as the sun god Apollo. Emperors were buried in its vaults until about AD 271, when under threat of invasion from Germanic raiders it became a citadel and was incorporated into the city's walls. Its present name arose in AD 590, after a vision by Gregory the Great, who while leading a procession through Rome to pray for the end of plague saw an angel sheathing a sword on this spot, an act thought to symbolize the end of the pestilence.

Castle and museum In AD 847 Leo IV converted the building into a papal fortress, and in 1277 Nicholas III linked it to the Vatican by a (still visible) passageway, the *passetto*. A prison in the Renaissance, and then an army barracks after 1870, the castle became a museum in 1933. Exhibits are spread over four floors, scattered around a confusing but fascinating array of rooms and corridors. Best of these is the beautiful Sala Paolina, decorated with stucco, fresco, and *trompe-l'oeil*. The most memorable sight is the 360° view from the castle's terrace, the setting for the last act of Puccini's *Tosca*.

HIGHLIGHTS

- Spiral funerary ramp
- Staircase of Alexander VI
- Armory
- Hall of Justice
- Fresco: *Justice*, attributed to Domenico Zaga
- Chapel of Leo X: facade by Michelangelo
- Sale di Clemente VII with wall paintings
- Cortile del Pozzo: wellhead
- Prisons (Prigione Storiche)
- Sala Paolina
- View from Loggia of Paul III

INFORMATION

- ✚ dI; C5
- ✉ Lungotevere Castello 50
- ☎ 06 687 5036/06 681 9111
- ◷ Tue–Sun 9–7
- 🍴 Café
- Ⓜ Lepanto
- 🚌 23, 54, 87, 280 to Lungotevere Castello, or 34, 49, 70, 81, 186, 926, 990 to Piazza Cavour
- ♿ Poor
- 💰 Expensive
- ↔ St. Peter's (▶ 24), Vatican Museums (▶ 25), Sistine Chapel (▶ 26), Piazza Navona (▶ 30), Altar of Peace (▶ 31)

A Bernini angel on the Ponte Sant'Angelo

5

SANTA MARIA IN TRASTEVERE

INFORMATION

- ✚ dIV; C6
- ✉ Piazza Santa Maria in Trastevere
- ☎ 06 581 4802
- 🕐 Daily 7:30–12:30, 4–7
- 🚌 8, 44, 56, 60, 75, 97, 170, 280, 710, 718, 719, 774, 780 to Viale di Trastevere, or 23, 65 to Lungotevere Raffaello Sanzio
- ♿ Wheelchair accessible
- ✋ Free

One of the most memorable sights of nighttime Rome is the 12th-century gold mosaics adorning the facade of Santa Maria in Trastevere, their floodlit glow casting a gentle light over the milling nocturnal crowds in the piazza below.

Early church Santa Maria in Trastevere is among the oldest officially sanctioned places of worship in Rome. It was reputedly founded in AD 222, allegedly on the spot where a fountain of olive oil had sprung from the earth on the day of Christ's birth (symbolizing the coming of the grace of God). Much of the present church was built in the 12th century during the reign of Innocent II, a member of the Papareschi, a prominent Trastevere family. Inside, the main colonnade of the nave is composed of reused and ancient Roman columns. The portico, containing fragments of Roman reliefs and inscriptions and medieval remains, was added in 1702 by Carlo Fontana, who was also responsible for the fountain that graces the adjoining piazza.

Mosaics The facade mosaics probably date from the mid-12th century, and depict the Virgin and Child with ten lamp-carrying companions. Long believed to portray the parable of the Wise and Foolish Virgins, their subject matter is now contested, as several "virgins" appear to be men and only two are carrying unlighted lamps (not the five of the parable). The mosaics of the upper apse inside the church, devoted to the glorification of the Virgin, date from the same period and represent Byzantine-influenced works by Greek or Greek-trained craftsmen. Those below, depicting scenes from the life of the Virgin (1291), are by the mosaicist and fresco painter Pietro Cavallini.

CAMPO DE' FIORI

There is nowhere more relaxing in Rome to sit down with a cappuccino and watch the world go by than Campo de' Fiori, a lovely old piazza whose fruit, vegetable, and fish market makes it one of the liveliest and most colorful corners of the old city.

Ancient square Campo de' Fiori—the "Field of Flowers"—was turned in the Middle Ages from a meadow facing the ancient Theater of Pompey (55 BC; now Palazzo Pio Righetti) into one of the city's most exclusive residential and business districts. By the 15th century it was surrounded by busy inns and bordellos, some run by the infamous courtesan Vannozza Catanei, mistress of the Borgia pope, Alexander VI. By 1600 it had also become a place of execution: Giordano Bruno was burned for heresy on the spot marked by his cowled statue.

Present day Students, foreigners, and tramps mingle with market vendors shouting their wares. Cafés, bars, and the wonderfully dingy wine bar at No. 15 have you reveling in street life. One block south lies Piazza Farnese, dominated by the Palazzo Farnese, a Renaissance masterpiece partly designed by Michelangelo and begun in 1516. It is now home to the French Embassy. One block west is the Palazzo della Cancelleria (1485), once the papal chancellery. The nearby Via Giulia, Via dei

Knife grinder

Baullari, the busy Via dei Cappellari, and Via del Pellegrino are all wonderful to explore.

HIGHLIGHTS

- Street market
- Wine bar Vineria Reggio
- Statue of Giordano Bruno
- Palazzo Farnese, Piazza Farnese
- Palazzo della Cancelleria, Piazza della Cancelleria
- Palazzo Pio Righetti
- Via Giulia
- Santa Maria dell'Orazione e Morte: church door decorated in stone skulls
- Via dei Baullari

INFORMATION

- ✚ eIII; C6
- ✉ Piazza Campo de' Fiori
- 🕐 Market Mon–Sat 7–1:30
- 🚌 46, 62, 64 to Corso Vittorio Emanuele II; or 8, 44, 56, 60, 65, 75, 170 to Via Arenula
- ♿ Cobbled streets and some curbs around piazza
- 🖐 Free
- ↔ Piazza Navona (➤ 30), Palazzo Spada (➤ 53), Fontana delle Tartarughe (➤ 55)

7

PIAZZA NAVONA

HIGHLIGHTS

- Fontana dei Quattro Fiumi
- Fontana del Moro (south)
- Fontana del Nettuno (north)
- Sant'Agnese in Agone
- Palazzo Pamphili
- San Luigi dei Francesi (Via Santa Giovanna d'Arco)
- Santa Maria della Pace (Vicolo dell'Arco della Pace 5)
- Santa Maria dell'Anima (Via della Pace)

INFORMATION

➕ el; C5

✉ Piazza Navona

Sant'Agnese in Agone

☎ 06 679 4435 ⏰ Mon–Sat 5PM–6:30PM; Sun 10–1

San Luigi dei Francesi

☎ 06 6880 3629 ⏰ Mon–Wed, Fri, Sat 8–12:30, 3:30–7; Thu, Sun 8–12:30

Santa Maria della Pace (cloister)

☎ 06 686 1156 ⏰ Tue–Sat 10–12, 4–6; Sun 9–11

Santa Maria dell'Anima

☎ 06 683 3729 ⏰ Mon–Sat 7:30–7; Sun 8–1, 3–7

🚇 Spagna

🚌 70, 81, 87, 186, 492 to Corso del Rinascimento, or 46, 62, 64 to Corso Vittorio Emanuele II

♿ Good (Santa Maria della Pace: two steps)

🎫 Free to piazza and churches

↔ Castel Sant'Angelo (➤ 27), Campo de' Fiori (➤ 29), Pantheon (➤ 33)

Piazza di Spagna may be more elegant and Campo de' Fiori more vivid, but the Piazza Navona, with its atmospheric echoes of a 2,000-year history, is a glorious place to amble, watch the world, and stop for a drink at a sun-drenched table.

History Piazza Navona owes its unmistakable elliptical shape to a stadium and racetrack built here in AD 86 by the Emperor Domitian. From the Circus Agonalis—the stadium for athletic games—comes the piazza's present name, rendered in medieval Latin as *in agone*, and then in Rome's strangulated dialect as *'n 'agona*. The stadium was used until well into the Middle Ages for festivals and competitions. The square owes its present appearance to its rebuilding by Pope Innocent X in 1644.

Around the piazza Bernini's Fontana dei Quattro Fiumi (1651), the "Fountain of the Four Rivers" (➤ 54), dominates. On the west side is the baroque Sant' Agnese (1652–57), whose facade was designed by Borromini. Beside it stands the Palazzo Pamphili, commissioned by Innocent X and now the Brazilian Embassy. Further afield, San Luigi dei Francesi is famous for three superlative Caravaggio paintings, and Santa Maria della Pace for a cloister by Bramante and Raphael's frescoes of the four Sybils.

Fontana dei Quattro Fiumi

ARA PACIS AUGUSTAE

Few ancient bas-reliefs are as beautiful or as striking as those on the marble screens protecting the Altar of Peace, painstakingly but triumphantly reconstructed and restored in its present position from disparate fragments over many years.

Monument to peace Now sheltered from Rome's marble-rotting pollution by a glass pavilion, the Ara Pacis Augustae (Altar of Peace) was built between 13 and 9 BC on the orders of the Senate as a memorial to the military victories in Gaul and Spain of the Emperor Augustus, and in celebration of the peace (*pacis*) he brought to the Empire after years of conquest and civil war. Its panels were buried or dispersed over the centuries; the first fragments were recovered in the 16th century, the last over 300 years later (some were found as far away as Paris).

Reliefs While the altar at the heart of the monument is comparatively plain, the walls around it are covered with finely carved bas-reliefs. The best occupy the exterior north and south walls: they depict processional scenes of the altar's consecration and show the family of Augustus (including his wife, Livia) with 12 *lictors* (with their rods, or *fasces*, symbols of authority) and four *flamine* (who lit the sacred fires tended in the Forum by the Vestal Virgins). Other scenes include the Lupercalium—the grotto where the she-wolf suckled Romulus and Remus—and Aeneas sacrificing the sow (both west panel), and the earth goddess Tellus (east panel). The delicate ornamentation below includes floral motifs. Nearby is the Piazza del Popolo, with monuments ranging from a 3,000-year-old Egyptian obelisk to twin baroque churches and a 16th-century gateway.

HIGHLIGHTS

- Emperor Augustus and family (south wall)
- Emperor Augustus and family (north wall)
- Aeneas sacrificing the sow
- Lupercalium
- Earth goddess Tellus
- Mausoleum of Augustus (Piazza Augusto Imperatore), to the east
- Piazza del Popolo
- Santa Maria di Montesanto and Santa Maria dei Miracoli (Piazza del Popolo)
- Egyptian obelisk (Piazza del Popolo)
- Porta del Popolo (Piazza del Popolo)

INFORMATION

- el; D5
- Via di Ripetta–Lungotevere in Augusto
- 06 6880 6848
- Summer: Tue–Sat 9–7; Sun 9–1. Winter: Tue–Sat 9–4:30; Sun 9–1
- 81, 926 to Lungotevere in Augusta and Via di Ripetta, or 119 to Via di Ripetta
- Poor
- Moderate
- Santa Maria del Popolo (► 32), Pantheon (► 33), Piazza di Spagna and Spanish Steps (► 40)

SANTA MARIA DEL POPOLO

HIGHLIGHTS

- Cappella Chigi
- *Conversion of St. Paul* and *Crucifixion of St. Peter*, Caravaggio
- *Coronation of the Virgin*, Pinturicchio
- Tombs of Ascanio Sforza and Girolamo Basso della Rovere
- *Nativity*, Pinturicchio
- Fresco: *Life of San Girolamo*, Tiberio d'Assisi
- *Delphic Sybil*, Pinturicchio
- Altar, Andrea Bregno
- Stained glass
- *Assumption of the Virgin*, Annibale Carracci

INFORMATION

Santa Maria del Popolo's appeal stems from its intimate size and location, and from a wonderfully varied and rich collection of works of art that ranges from masterpieces by Caravaggio to some of Rome's earliest stained-glass windows.

Renaissance achievement Founded in 1099 on the site of Nero's grave, Santa Maria del Popolo was rebuilt by Pope Sixtus IV in 1472 and extended later by Bramante and Bernini. The right nave's first chapel, the Cappella della Rovere, is decorated with frescoes—*Life of San Girolamo* (1485–90)—by Tiberio d'Assisi, a pupil of Pinturicchio whose *Nativity* (c1490) graces the chapel's main altar. A doorway in the right transept leads to the sacristy, noted for its elaborate marble altar (1473) by Andrea Bregno.

Apse The apse contains two fine stained-glass windows (1509) by the French artist Guillaume de Marcillat. On either side are the greatest of the church's monuments: the tombs of the cardinals Ascanio Sforza (1505, left) and Girolamo Basso della Rovere (1507, right). Both are the work of Andrea Sansovino. High on the walls are superb and elegant frescoes (1508–10) of the Virgin, Evangelists, the Fathers of the Church, and Sybils by Pinturicchio.

North nave The frescoed first chapel, the Cappella Cerasi, also contains three major paintings: the altarpiece, *Assumption of the Virgin*, by Annibale Carracci (above); and Caravaggio's dramatic *Conversion of St. Paul* and the *Crucifixion of St. Peter* (all 1601). The famous Cappella Chigi (1513) was commissioned by the wealthy Sienese banker Agostino Chigi, while its architecture, sculpture, and paintings were designed as a unified whole by Raphael.

PANTHEON

No other monument suggests the grandeur of ancient Rome as magnificently as the Pantheon, a temple whose early conversion to a place of Christian worship has rendered it the most perfect of the city's ancient monuments.

Temple and church Built by the Emperor Hadrian from AD 118–28, the Pantheon replaced a temple of 27 BC by Marcus Agrippa, son-in-law of Augustus (modestly, Hadrian retained the original inscription proclaiming it as Agrippa's work). It became the church of Santa Maria ad Martyres in AD 609 (the bones of martyrs were brought here from the Catacombs) and is now a shrine to Italy's "immortals," including the artist Raphael and kings Vittore Emanuele II and Umberto I.

An engineering marvel Massive and simple externally, the Pantheon is even more breathtaking inside, where the scale, harmony, and symmetry of the dome in particular are more apparent. The world's largest dome until 1882 (when it was surpassed in the English spa resort of Buxton), it has a diameter of 142 feet—equal to its height from the floor. Weight and stresses were reduced by rows of coffering in the ceiling, and the use of progressively lighter materials from the base to the crown. The central oculus, 29 feet in diameter and clearly intended to inspire meditation on the heavens above, lets light (and rain) fall onto the marble pavement far below.

HIGHLIGHTS

- Façade inscription
- The pedimented portico
- Original Roman doors
- Marble interior and pavement
- Coffered dome and oculus
- Tomb of Raphael
- Royal tombs

INFORMATION

- ✚ ell; D5
- ✉ Piazza della Rotonda
- ☎ 06 6830 0230
- 🕐 Apr–Sep: Mon–Sat 9–6:30; Sun 9–1. Oct–Mar: Mon–Sat 9–5; Sun 9–1
- Ⓢ Spagna
- 🚌 119 to Piazza della Rotonda, or 64, 70, 75 and all other services to Largo di Torre Argentina
- ♿ Good
- 🆓 Free
- ↔ Piazza Navona (➤ 30), Santa Maria sopra Minerva (➤ 34)

The Pantheon

11

SANTA MARIA SOPRA MINERVA

HIGHLIGHTS

- Egyptian obelisk atop an elephant, Bernini (outside)
- Porch to the Cappella Carafa
- Frescoes: *St. Thomas Aquinas* and *The Assumption*, Filippino Lippi, in the Cappella Carafa
- *Risen Christ*, Michelangelo
- Relics of St. Catherine of Siena, and preserved room in sacristy where she died
- Tombs of Clement VII and Leo X, Antonio da Sangallo
- Tomb-slab of Fra Angelico
- Tomb of Giovanni Alberini, Mino da Fiesole or Agostino di Duccio
- Monument to Maria Raggi
- Tomb of Francesco Tornabuoni, Mino da Fiesole

INFORMATION

- ✚ fII, D5
- ✉ Piazza della Minerva 42
- ☎ 06 679 3926
- 🕐 Daily 7–12, 4–7
- Ⓜ Spagna
- 🚌 44, 46, 56, 60, 61, 64, 65, 70, 75, 81, 87, 90, 170 to Largo di Torre Argentina, or 119 to Piazza della Rotonda
- ♿ Stepped access to church
- 💲 Free
- ↔ Pantheon (➤ 33), Palazzo-Galleria Doria Pamphili (➤ 36), Fontana di Trevi (➤ 39)

Remarkable in having steadfastly retained many Gothic features despite Rome's love for the baroque, behind its plain facade Santa Maria sopra Minerva is a cornucopia of tombs, paintings, and Renaissance sculpture.

Florentine influences Originally founded in the 8th century over ruins of a temple to Minerva, the church was built in 1280 to a design by a pair of Florentine Dominican monks who modeled it on their own church, Santa Maria Novella.

Interior The interior of the church abounds with beautiful works such as the Cappella Carafa (whose fine porch is attributed to Giuliano da Maiano),

Elephant supporting an obelisk, by Bernini

and Michelangelo's calm statue *The Risen Christ* (1521), left of the high altar. Filippino Lippi painted the celebrated frescoes *St. Thomas Aquinas* and the *Assumption* (1488–93). Among other sculptures are the tombs of Francesco Tornabuoni (1480) and that of Giovanni Alberini, the latter decorated with reliefs of Hercules (15th century). Both are attributed to Mino da Fiesole. Other works include Fra Angelico's tomb slab (1455); the tombs of Medici popes Clement VII and Leo X (1536) by Antonio da Sangallo the Younger; and Bernini's monument to Maria Raggi (1643). St. Catherine of Siena, one of Italy's patron saints, is buried beneath the high altar.

VILLA GIULIA

The Museo Nazionale di Villa Giulia houses the world's greatest collection of Etruscan art and artifacts. The exhibits may not always be perfectly presented, but it is a revelation to discover the mysterious civilization that preceded ancient Rome.

The villa Built in 1550–55 as a country house and garden for the hedonistic Pope Julius III, the Villa Giulia was designed by some of the leading architects of the day, including Michelangelo and Georgio Vasari. Restoration has rescued the frescoed loggia and the Nymphaeum, a sunken court in the gardens by the Mannerist architect Giacomo da Vignola.

The collection The exhibits, which range over two floors and 34 rooms, are generally divided between finds from Etruscan sites in northern Etruria (western central Italy, including Vulci, Veio, Cerveteri, and Tarquinia) and from excavations in the south (Nemi and Praeneste), including artifacts made by the Greeks. Most notable are the Castellani exhibits, which include vases, cups, and ewers, and jewelry from the Minoan period (the latter collection is one of the villa's special treasures). To see the most striking works of art, be selective. Pick through the numerous vases, and note the *Tomba del Guerriero* and the *Cratere a Volute*. Note also the *Sarcofago degli Sposi*, a 6th-century BC sarcophagus with figures of a married couple reclining together on a banqueting couch; the engraved marriage coffer known as the *Cista Ficoroni* (4th century BC); the giant terra-cotta figures, *Hercules and Apollo*; the temple sculptures from Falerii Veteres; and the valuable 7th-century BC relics in gold, silver, bronze, and ivory from the Barberini and Bernardini tombs in Praeneste, 24 miles east of Rome.

HIGHLIGHTS

- *Lamine d'Oro*, Sala di Pyrgi: a gold tablet (left of entrance)
- Vase: *Tomba del Guerriero* (room 4)
- Terra-cottas: *Hercules and Apollo* (room 7)
- *Sarcofago degli Sposi* (room 9)
- Castellani Collection (rooms 19–22)
- Vase: *Cratere a Volute* (room 26)
- Finds from Falerii Veteres (room 29)
- Tomb relics: Barberini and Bernardini (room 33)
- Marriage coffer: *Cista Ficoroni* (room 33)
- Gardens with Nymphaeum and reconstructed "Temple of Alatri"

INFORMATION

- ✚ D3
- ✉ Piazzale di Villa Giulia 9
- ☎ 06 322 6571/06 320 1951
- 🕐 Tue–Sat 9–7; Sun 9–1:30
- 🍴 Café and shop
- Ⓜ Flaminio
- 🚌 52, 926 to Viale Bruno Buozzi, or 95, 490, 495 to Viale Washington
- ♿ Good
- 💲 Expensive
- ↔ Santa Maria del Popolo (► 32), Galleria Borghese (► 45)

13

PALAZZO-GALLERIA DORIA PAMPHILI

HIGHLIGHTS

- *Religion Succored by Spain* (labeled 10) and *Salome* (29), Titian
- *Portrait of Two Venetians* (23), Raphael
- *Maddalena* (40) and *Rest on the Flight into Egypt* (42), Caravaggio
- *Birth* and *Marriage of the Virgin* (174/176), Giovanni di Paolo
- *Nativity* (200), Parmigianino
- *Innocent X*, Velázquez
- *Innocent X*, Bernini
- *Battle of the Bay of Naples* (317), Pieter Brueghel the Elder
- Salone Verde
- Saletta Gialla

INFORMATION

- ✚ fII; D6
- ✉ Piazza del Collegio Romano 1a
- ☎ 06 679 7323
- 🕐 Fri–Wed 10–5. Apartments Fri–Wed 10:30–12:30. Closed public hols
- 🚇 Barberini
- 🚌 56, 60, 62, 85, 95, 160, 492 to Piazza Venezia
- ♿ Good
- 💶 Gallery expensive. Apartments moderate
- ↔ Pantheon (➤ 33), Santa Maria sopra Minerva (➤ 34), Capitoline Museums (➤ 37), Santa Maria in Aracoeli (➤ 38), Fontana di Trevi (➤ 39)

The Palazzo Doria Pamphili is among the largest of Rome's palaces, and is still privately owned. It contains one of the city's finest patrician art collections and offers the chance to admire some of the sumptuously decorated rooms of its private apartments.

Palace Little in the bland exterior of the Palazzo Doria Pamphili prepares you for the splendor of the beautifully decorated rooms that lie within. The core of the building, which was built over the foundations of a storehouse dating back to classical times, was erected in 1435, and it has withstood countless alterations and owners. The Doria Pamphili dynasty was formed by yoking together the Doria, a famous Genoese seafaring clan, and the Pamphili, an ancient Rome-based patrician family. Most people come here for the paintings, but for an additional fee you can enjoy a guided tour around some of the private apartments in the 1,000-room palace. The most impressive is the Saletta Gialla (Yellow Room), decorated with 12 Gobelin tapestries made for Louis XV. In the Salone Verde (Green Room) are three important paintings: *Annunciation* by Filippo Lippi, *Portrait of a Gentleman* by Lorenzo Lotto, and *Andrea Doria* (a famous admiral) by Sebastiano del Piombo.

Paintings The Pamphili's splendid art collection is displayed in ranks in four broad galleries. Because the works are numbered, not labeled, it's worthwhile to invest in a catalog from the ticket office. The finest painting by far is the famous Velázquez portrait, *Innocent X*, a likeness that captured the pope's weak and suspicious nature so adroitly that Innocent is said to have lamented that it was "too true, too true." The nearby bust by Bernini of the same pope is more flattering.

MUSEI CAPITOLINI

Few in number, but outstanding, the Greek and Roman sculptures in the Capitoline Museums (Palazzo Nuovo and Palazzo dei Conservatori) make a far more accessible introduction to the subject than the Vatican Museums.

Palazzo Nuovo The Capitoline Museums occupy two palaces on opposite sides of the Piazza del Campidoglio. Designed by Michelangelo, the Palazzo Nuovo (on the north side) contains most of the finest pieces, none greater than the magnificent 2nd-century AD bronze equestrian statue of Marcus Aurelius (just off the main courtyard). Moved here from outside San Giovanni in Laterano in the Middle Ages, it is now restored and covered. Among the sculptures inside are celebrated Roman copies in marble of Greek originals, including the *Dying Gaul*, *Wounded Amazon*, *Capitoline Venus*, and the discus thrower *Discobolus* (➤ 52). In the Sala degli Imperatori is a portrait gallery of busts of Roman emperors.

Palazzo dei Conservatori This former seat of Rome's medieval magistrates contains an art gallery (the Pinacoteca Capitolina) on the third floor and a further rich hoard of classical sculpture on the second. Bronzes include the 1st-century BC *Spinario*, a boy removing a thorn from his foot, and the 5th-century BC Etruscan *Lupa Capitolina*, the famous she-wolf suckling Romulus and Remus (the twins were added by Antonio Pollaiuolo in 1510). Paintings in the Pinacoteca include *St. John the Baptist* by Caravaggio and works by Velázquez, Titian, Veronese, and Van Dyck.

HIGHLIGHTS

Palazzo Nuovo
● Statue of Marcus Aurelius
● Sculpture: *Capitoline Venus*
● Sculpture: *Dying Gaul*
● Sculpture: *Wounded Amazon*
● Sculpture: *Discobolus*
● Sala degli Imperatori

Palazzo dei Conservatori
● St. John the Baptist, Caravaggio
● Bronze: *Capitoline Wolf*
● Bronze: *Spinario*
● Marble figure: *Esquiline Venus*

INFORMATION

➕ fIV–gIV; D6
✉ Musei Capitolini (Capitoline Museums), Piazza del Campidoglio 1
☎ 06 6710 2071
🕐 Tue–Sat 9–7; Sun 9–1:30. Closed Aug 15–31
🚌 44, 46, 64, 70, 81, 110 and all services to Piazza Venezia
♿ Poor: stepped ramp to Piazza del Campidoglio
💷 Expensive (free last Sun of month)
🔄 Santa Maria in Aracoeli (➤ 38), Roman Forum (➤ 41)

Statue of Constantine, Palazzo dei Conservatori

15

Santa Maria in Aracoeli

HIGHLIGHTS

- Aracoeli staircase
- Wooden ceiling
- Cosmati pavement
- Nave columns
- Tomb of Cardinal d'Albret, Andrea Bregno
- Tomb of Giovanni Crivelli, Donatello
- Frescoes: *Life of St. Bernardino of Siena*
- Tomb of Luca Savelli, attributed to Arnolfo di Cambio
- Tomb of Filippo Della Valle, attributed to Andrea Briosco
- Fresco: *St. Anthony of Padua*, Benozzo Gozzoli

INFORMATION

- ✚ fIII; D6
- ✉ Piazza d'Aracoeli
- ☎ 06 679 8155
- ◷ Jun–Sep: daily 7 or 8–noon, 4–6:30. Oct–May: daily 7–noon
- 🚌 44, 46, 56, 60, 64, 65, 70, 75, 170, 492 and all other services to Piazza Venezia
- ♿ Poor: steep steps to main entrance or steps to Piazza del Campidoglio
- 🎫 Free
- ↔ Palazzo-Galleria Doria Pamphili (➤ 36), Capitoline Museums (➤ 37), Roman Forum (➤ 41)

Perched atop the Capitoline Hill—long one of Rome's most sacred spots—Santa Maria in Aracoeli, with its glorious ceiling, fine frescoes, and soft chandelier-lit interior, makes a calm retreat from the ferocious traffic and hurrying crowds of Piazza Venezia.

Approach There are 124 steep steps in Santa Maria's staircase, built in 1348 to celebrate either the end of a plague epidemic or the Holy Year proclaimed for 1350. Today it is traditionally climbed by newly married couples.

Ancient foundation The church was first recorded in AD 574, but even then it was old. Emperor Augustus raised an altar here, the Ara Coeli (the Altar of Heaven), with the inscription now on the church's triumphal arch: *Ecce ara primogeniti Dei* (Behold the altar of the firstborn of God). Most of the present structure dates from 1260.

Interior Although only one work of art stands out (Pinturicchio's frescoes, the *Life of St. Bernardino of Siena*, 1486), the overall sense is of grandeur, achieved by virtue of the gilded ceiling

(installed between 1572 and 1575 to celebrate a naval victory over the Turks in 1571), and by the nave's enormous columns, removed from lost ancient buildings. Tombs to see include those of Cardinal d'Albret, Giovanni Crivelli, Luca Savelli, and Filippo Della Valle.

Detail from the Life of St. Bernardino of Siena

FONTANA DI TREVI

There is no lovelier surprise in Rome than that which suddenly confronts you as you emerge from the tight warren of streets around the Fontana di Trevi, the city's most famous fountain—a sight "silvery to the eye and ear," in the words of Charles Dickens.

Virgin discovery In its earliest guise the Fontana di Trevi lay at the end of the Aqua Virgo, or Acqua Vergine, an aqueduct built by Agrippa in 19 BC (supposedly filled with Rome's sweetest waters). The spring that fed it was reputedly discovered by a virgin, hence its name. (She is said to have shown her discovery to some Roman soldiers, a scene—along with Agrippa's approval of the aqueduct's plans—described in bas-reliefs on the fountain's second tier.) The fountain's liveliness and charm is embodied in the pose of *Oceanus*, the central figure, and the two giant tritons and their horses (symbolizing a calm and a stormy sea) drawing his chariot. Other statues represent Abundance and Health and, above, the Four Seasons, which each carry gifts.

Fountains A new fountain was built in 1453 on the orders of Pope Nicholas V, who paid for it by levying a tax on wine—Romans sneered that he "took our wine to give us water." Its name came from the three roads (*tre vie*) that converged on the piazza. The present fountain was commissioned by Pope Clement XII in 1732 and finished 30 years later: its design was inspired by the Arch of Constantine and is attributed to Nicola Salvi, with possible contributions from Bernini (though the most audacious touch—combining a fountain with a palace-like facade—was probably the work of Pietro da Cortona). Visitors wishing to return to Rome throw a coin (preferably over the shoulder) into the fountain. The money goes to the Italian Red Cross.

HIGHLIGHTS

- *Oceanus* (Neptune)
- *Allegory of Health* (right of *Oceanus*)
- *Virgin Indicating the Spring to Soldiers*
- *Allegory of Abundance* (left of *Oceanus*)
- *Agrippa Approving the Design of the Aqueduct*
- *Triton with Horse* (on the right, symbolizing the ocean in repose)
- *Triton with Horse* (on the left, symbolizing a tempestuous sea)
- Facade of Santi Vincenzo e Anastasio
- Baroque interior of Santa Maria in Trivio

INFORMATION

- fII–gII; D5
- Piazza Fontana di Trevi
- Always open
- Spagna or Barberini
- 52, 53, 56, 58, 60, 61, 62, and other routes to Via del Corso and Via del Tritone
- Access via cobbled street
- Free
- Pantheon (➤ 33), Santa Maria sopra Minerva (➤ 34), Palazzo-Galleria Doria Pamphili (➤ 36), Piazza di Spagna & Spanish Steps (➤ 40)

PIAZZA DI SPAGNA & SPANISH STEPS

HIGHLIGHTS

- Spanish Steps
- Museo Keats–Shelley (➤ 52)
- Trinità dei Monti
- Fontana della Barcaccia (➤ 54)
- Babington's Tea Rooms (➤ 69)
- Caffè Greco (➤ 69)
- Villa Medici gardens
- Pincio Gardens (➤ 57)

INFORMATION

- ✚ fl–gl; D5
- ✉ Piazza di Spagna
- ☎ Museo Keats–Shelley 06 678 4235. Babington's Tea Rooms 06 678 6027. Caffè Greco 06 678 5474. Villa Medici 06 679 8381
- 🕐 Spanish Steps always open. Museo Keats–Shelley Mon–Fri 9–1, 3–6. Trinità dei Monti daily 10–12:30, 4–6. Villa Medici occasionally open for exhibitions. Gardens apply to the French Academy
- 🍴 Caffè Greco, Babington's Tea Rooms (➤ 69)
- 🚇 Spagna
- 🚌 119 to Piazza di Spagna
- ♿ None for the Spanish Steps
- 💷 Free except to Museo Keats–Shelley (moderate)
- ↔ Santa Maria del Popolo (➤ 32), Palazzo Barberini (➤ 42)

Neither old nor particularly striking, the Spanish Steps are nonetheless one of Rome's most famous sights, thanks largely to their popularity as a meeting point, to their views, and to their position at the heart of the city's most exclusive shopping district.

Spanish Steps Despite their name, the Spanish Steps were commissioned by a Frenchman, Étienne Gueffier (the French ambassador), who in 1723 sought to link Piazza di Spagna with the French-owned church of Trinità dei Monti on the hill above. A century earlier the piazza had housed the headquarters of the Spanish ambassador to the Holy See, hence the name of both the steps and the square.

Around the steps At the base of the steps is the Fontana della Barcaccia, commissioned in 1627 by Urban VIII and designed either by Gian Lorenzo Bernini or by his less famous father, Pietro. The eccentric design represents a half-sunken boat (➤ 54). As you face the steps from below, to your right stands the Museo Keats–Shelley (➤ 52), a fascinating collection of literary memorabilia and a working library housed in the lodgings where the poet John Keats died in 1821. To the left are the famed Babington's Tea Rooms (➤ 69) and to the south the Via Condotti, Rome's most exclusive shopping street. At the top of the steps you can enjoy views past the Palazzo Barberini and towards the Quirinal Hill; walk into the simple Trinità dei Monti, with its outside double-staircase by Domenico Fontana; and visit the beautiful gardens of the 16th-century Villa Medici (generally open Sunday morning only), the seat of the French Academy in Rome, where scholars study painting, sculpture, architecture, engraving, and music.

FORO ROMANO

The civic and political heart of the Roman Empire was the Roman Forum. Its ruins can be difficult to decipher, but the site is one of the most evocative in the city, the standing stones and fragments conjuring up echoes of a once all-powerful state.

History The Forum (Foro Romano) started life as a marsh between the Palatine and Capitoline hills, taking its name from a word meaning "outside the walls." Later it became a rubbish dump, and, having been drained, a marketplace and a religious shrine. In time it acquired all the structures of Rome's burgeoning civic, social, and political life. Over the centuries consuls, emperors, and senators embellished it with magnificent temples, courts, and basilicas.

Forum and Palatine Two millennia of plunder and decay have left a mish-mash of odd pillars and jumbled stones, which nonetheless can begin to make vivid sense given a plan and some imagination. This strange, empty space is romantic, especially on the Palatine Hill to the south, once covered by a palace. Today orange trees, oleanders, and cypresses line the paths; grasses and wildflowers flourish among the ancient remains. Worth a visit are the Temple of Antoninus and Faustina, the Colonna di Foca, the Curia, the restored Arch of Septimius Severus, the Portico of the Dei Consentes, the Temple of Saturn, Santa Maria Antiqua (the oldest church in the Forum), the House of the Vestal Virgins (who tended the sacred fire), the aisle of the Basilica of the Emperor Maxentius, and the Arch of Titus.

HIGHLIGHTS

- Temple of Antoninus and Faustina (Tempio di Antonino e Faustina, AD 141, a church in medieval times)
- Colonna di Foca (AD 608)
- Curia (Senate House, 80 BC)
- Arch of Septimius Severus (Arco di Settimio Severo, AD 203)
- 12 columns from the Portico of the Dei Consentes (AD 367)
- 8 columns from the Temple of Saturn (Tempio di Saturno, 42 BC, AD 284)
- House of the Vestal Virgins

INFORMATION

- ✚ gIV; D6–E6
- ✉ Entrances at Portale del Vignola at the Arch of Constantine, Arco di Tito and Largo Romolo e Remo on Via dei Fori Imperiali
- ☎ 06 699 0110
- 🕐 Tue–Sat 9 to 1 hour before dusk; Sun, Mon 9–2
- 🚇 Colosseo
- 🚌 11, 27, 81, 85, 87, 186 to Via dei Fori Imperiali
- ♿ Access only from Largo Romolo e Remo
- 🎫 Forum free. Palatine expensive
- ↔ Capitoline Museums (➤ 37), Colosseum (➤ 43), San Clemente (➤ 46), Arch of Constantine (➤ 50)

Pillar and capital from the Forum

19

PALAZZO BARBERINI

HIGHLIGHTS

- Central windows and Scala Elicoidale
- *Madonna and Child* and *Annunciation*, Filippo Lippi (room II)
- *Holy Family* and *Madonna and Saints*, Andrea del Sarto (room V)
- *Madonna and Child*, Beccafumi (room V)
- *La Fornarina*, Raphael (room VI)
- *Adoration of the Shepherds* and *Baptism of Christ*, El Greco (room IX)
- *Judith and Holofernes* and *Narciso*, Caravaggio (room XIV)
- *Beatrice Cenci*, attributed to Guido Reni (room XVIII)
- *Henry VIII*, attributed to Holbein (room XIX)
- *The Triumph of Divine Providence*, Pietro da Cortona (Gran Salone)

INFORMATION

- ✚ hI; E5
- ✉ Via delle Quattro Fontane 13
- ☎ 06 481 4591/06 482 4184
- 🕐 Tue–Sun 9–7; hols 9–1
- Ⓜ Barberini
- 🚍 52, 53, 56, 58, 58b, 60, 95, 119, 492 to Via del Tritone, or 57, 64, 65, 70, 71, 75, 170 to Via Nazionale
- ♿ Few
- 💰 Moderate
- ⇄ Piazza di Spagna (➤ 40), Santa Maria Maggiore (➤ 47)

The magnificent Palazzo Barberini—designed by Bernini, Borromini, and Carlo Maderno—also houses a stupendous ceiling fresco and one of Rome's finest art collections, the Galleria Nazionale d'Arte Antica (the earlier works of the national art collection).

Urban's splendor The palace was commissioned by Maffeo Barberini for his family when he became Pope Urban VIII in 1623. The epitome of Rome's high baroque style, it is a maze of suites, apartments, and staircases, many still swathed in their sumptuous original decoration. Overshadowing all is the Gran Salone, dominated by Pietro da Cortona's rich ceiling frescoes, glorifying Urban as an agent of Divine Providence. The central windows and oval spiral staircase (Scala Elicoidale) are the work of Borromini.

The collection *"Antica"* here means old rather than ancient. Probably the most popular painting in the collection is Raphael's *La Fornarina* (also attributed to Giulio Romano). It is reputedly a

portrait of one of the artist's several mistresses, identified later as the daughter of a *fornaio* (baker). It was executed in the year of the painter's death, a demise brought on, it is said, by his mistress's unrelenting passion. Elsewhere, eminent Italian works from Filippo Lippi, Andrea del Sarto, Caravaggio, and Guido Reni stand alongside paintings by leading foreign artists.

Raphael's La Fornarina

COLOSSEO

The Pantheon may be better preserved, and the Forum more historically important, but no other monument in Rome rivals the majesty of the Colosseum, the world's largest surviving structure from Roman antiquity.

History The Colosseum was begun by the Emperor Vespasian in AD 72 and inaugurated by his son, Titus, in AD 80 with a gala that saw 5,000 animals slaughtered in a day (and 100 days of continuous games thereafter). Finishing touches to the 55,000-seat stadium were added by Domitian (AD 81–96). Three types of columns support the arcades, and the walls are made of brick and volcanic tufa faced with marble blocks, which were once bound together by metal clamps (removed in AD 664). The long decline began in the Middle Ages, with the pillaging of stone to build churches and palaces. The desecration ended in 1744, when the structure was consecrated in memory of the Christians supposedly martyred in the arena (more recent research suggests they weren't). Clearing of the site and excavations began late in the 19th century and restoration was carried out in the 20th.

Games Armed combat at the Colosseum went on for some 500 years. Criminals, slaves, and gladiators fought each other or wild animals, often to the death. Women and dwarfs also wrestled, and mock sea battles were waged (the arena could be flooded via underground pipes). Spectators could exercise the power of life and death over defeated combatants, by waving handkerchiefs to show mercy, or by displaying a down-turned thumb to demand the finishing stroke. Survivors' throats were often cut anyway, and the dead were poked with red-hot irons to make sure they had actually expired.

HIGHLIGHTS

- Circumference walls
- Arches: 80 lower arches for the easy admission of crowds
- Doric columns: lowest arcade
- Ionic columns: central arcade
- Corinthian columns: upper arcade
- Underground cells for animals
- Sockets that once housed binding metal clamps
- *Vomitoria:* interior exits and entrances
- Views from the upper levels
- Arch of Constantine nearby (➤ 50)

INFORMATION

✚ hIV; E6

✉ Piazza del Colosseo, Via dei Fori Imperiali

☎ 06 700 4261

🕐 Tue–Sat 9–1 hour before dusk; Sun, Mon 9–2

🚇 Colosseo

🚍 11, 13, 15, 27, 30b, 81, 85, 87, 118, 186, 673 to Piazza del Colosseo

♿ Poor to the interior; limited access from Via Celio Vibenna entrance

💵 Ground floor free. Upper levels moderate

↔ Capitoline Museums (➤ 37), Roman Forum (➤ 41), San Pietro in Vincoli (➤ 44), San Clemente (➤ 46), Arch of Constantine (➤ 50)

21

SAN PIETRO IN VINCOLI

HIGHLIGHTS

- *Moses*, Michelangelo
- Profile self-portrait in the upper part of Moses' beard
- Chains of St. Peter
- Early Christian carved sarcophagus (crypt)
- Mosaic: *St. Sebastian*
- Tomb of Niccolò da Cusa
- *Santa Margherita*, Guercino
- Tomb of Antonio and Piero Pollaiuolo
- Torre dei Margani (Piazza San Pietro in Vincoli), once believed to have been owned by the Borgias

INFORMATION

- hIII; E6
- Piazza di San Pietro in Vincoli 4a
- 06 488 2865
- Apr–Sep: Mon–Sat 7–12:30, 3:30–7; Sun 8:45–11:30AM. Oct–Mar: Mon–Sat 7–12:30, 3:30–6; Sun 8:45–11:30AM
- Colosseo or Cavour
- 11, 27, 81 to Via Cavour, or 11, 27, 81, 85, 87, 186 to Piazza del Colosseo
- Good
- Free
- Roman Forum (➤ 41), Colosseum (➤ 43), Santa Maria Maggiore (➤ 47)

Hidden in a narrow back street, San Pietro in Vincoli is a thoroughly appealing church. Drop by for the chance to admire Michelangelo's statue of Moses, one of the most powerful of all the artist's monumental sculptures.

Chains San Pietro in Vincoli takes its name from the chains (*vincoli*) proudly clasped in the coffer with bronze doors under the high altar. According to tradition they are the chains used to bind St. Peter while he was held captive in the Mamertine prison (remnants of which are preserved under the church of San Giuseppe near the Forum). Part of the chains found their way to Constantinople, while the rest were housed in San Pietro by Pope Leo I (who had the church specially reconstructed from a 4th-century building for the purpose). When the two parts were eventually reunited, they are said to have miraculously fused together. The church has often been transformed and restored. The 20 columns of its interior arcade came originally from a Roman temple.

Works of art Michelangelo's majestic sculpture (of a patriarchal Moses receiving the Tablets of Stone) was originally designed as part of a 42-figure ensemble for the tomb of Julius II. Michelangelo spent years scouring the Carrara mountains for suitable pieces of stone, but the project never came close to completion, and he was to describe the work as "this tragedy of a tomb". Instead, much of his time was spent (reluctantly) on the Sistine Chapel. Also make sure you see the Byzantine mosaic *St. Sebastian* (*c*680), the monument to the Pollaiuolo brothers (*c*1498) by Luigi Capponi, and the tomb of Cardinal da Cusa (1464), attributed to the Lombard sculptor Andrea Bregno.

GALLERIA BORGHESE

The Galleria Borghese may be relatively small, but what it lacks in quantity it makes up for in quality. It combines paintings and sculptures, including many of the masterpieces of Gian Lorenzo Bernini and paintings by Raphael, Caravaggio and others.

Seductress The Villa Borghese was designed in 1613 as a summer retreat for Cardinal Scipione Borghese, nephew of Pope Paul V, who accumulated most of the collection (acquired by the state in 1902). Scipione was an enthusiastic patron of Bernini, whose works dominate the gallery. The museum's foremost masterpiece, however, is Antonio Canova's *Paolina Borghese* (above), Napoleon's sister, and wife of Camillo Borghese. Depicted bare-breasted, with a come-hither hauteur, Paolina was just as slyly seductive in life. Her jewels, her clothes, her lovers, and the servants she used as footstools all excited gossip.

Bernini His *David* (1623–4) is said to be a self-portrait, while *Apollo and Daphne* (1622–25), in the next room, is considered his masterpiece. Other Bernini works include the *Rape of Proserpine* (1622) and *Truth Unveiled by Time* (1652).

Temple of Aesculapius, Villa Borghese

The paintings Foremost in this wonderful collection are works by Raphael (*The Deposition of Christ*), Titian (*Sacred and Profane Love*), Caravaggio (*Boy with a Fruit Basket* and *Madonna dei Palafrenieri*), and Correggio (*Danae*).

HIGHLIGHTS

Galleria Borghese
- *Paolina Borghese*, Canova
- *David*, Bernini
- *Apollo and Daphne*, Bernini
- *Madonna dei Palafrenieri*, Caravaggio
- *Sacred and Profane Love*, Titian
- *Deposition of Christ*, Raphael

INFORMATION

Galleria Borghese
- ✚ E4
- ✉ Piazzale Scipione Borghese 5
- ☎ 06 841 7645
- 🕐 Tue–Sun 9–7. Closed public hols. Advance reservations are obligatory ☎ 06 328101
- 🚇 Spagna or Flaminio
- 🚌 52, 53, 910 to Via Pinciana, or 3, 4, 56, 57, 319 to Via Po, or 19, 30b to Via delle Belle Arti
- ♿ Steps to front entrance
- 💰 Moderate
- ↔ Villa Giulia (➤ 35), Piazza di Spagna & Spanish Steps (➤ 40), Palazzo Barberini (➤ 42)

SAN CLEMENTE

HIGHLIGHTS

- Choir screen
- Chapel of St. Catherine: fresco cycle
- Ciborio: altar canopy
- Apse mosaic: *The Triumph of the Cross*
- Monument to Cardinal Roverella, Giovanni Dalmata (upper church)
- Fresco: *Miracle of San Clemente*
- Fresco: *Legend of Sisinnio*
- Triclinium
- Altar of Mithras: bas-relief of Mithras slaying the bull

No site in Rome reveals as vividly the layers of history that underpin the city as San Clemente, a beautiful medieval ensemble built over a superbly preserved 4th-century church and the remains of a 3rd-century Mithraic temple.

Upper church The present San Clemente—named after Rome's fourth pope—was built between 1108 and 1184 to replace an earlier one that was sacked by the Normans in 1084. Almost untouched since, its medieval interior is dominated by the 12th-century marble panels of the choir screen and pulpits and the glittering 12th-century apse mosaic, *The Triumph of the Cross*. Equally captivating are the *Life of St. Catherine* frescoes (1428–31), by Masolino da Panicale.

Below ground Steps descend to the lower church, which retains traces of its 8th- to 11th-century frescoes of San Clemente, and

Mithraic temple

INFORMATION

- hIV; E6
- Via di San Giovanni in Laterano
- 06 7045 1018
- Apr–Sep: daily 9–12:30, 3:30–6:30. Oct–Mar: daily 9–12:30, 3:30–6
- 15, 81, 85, 87, 93, 118, 186 to Via Labicana, or 13, 30b to Colosseum
- Church free. Excavations inexpensive

the legends of SS Alessio and Sisinnio. More steps lead deeper into the twilight world of the best-preserved of the 12 Mithraic temples uncovered in Rome. (Mithraism was a popular, men-only cult, eclipsed by Christianity.) Here are an altar with a bas-relief of Mithras ritually slaying a bull, and the Triclinium, used for banquets and rites. Excavations are revealing parts of the temple, and the 1,900-year-old remains of other buildings, streets, and an underground stream which you can hear even today, that may have formed part of ancient Rome's drainage system.

SANTA MARIA MAGGIORE

Santa Maria Maggiore is Rome's finest early Christian basilica, thanks to its magnificent mosaic-swathed interior. It is also the only church in the city where mass has been celebrated every single day since the 5th century.

History According to myth, the Virgin appeared to Pope Liberius on August 5, AD 352, and told him to build a church exactly where snow would fall the next day. Although it was summer, the snow fell, marking the outlines of a basilica on the Esquiline Hill. Legend aside, the church probably dates from AD 430, though the campanile (the tallest in Rome at 246 feet) was added in 1377, and the interior and exterior were altered in the 13th and 18th centuries. The coffered ceiling, attributed to Giuliano da Sangallo, was reputedly gilded with the first gold to arrive from the New World, a gift from Spain to Alexander VI (note his Borgia bull emblems).

Interior Beyond the general splendor, the main treasures are the 36 mosaics in the architraves of the nave: 5th-century depictions of the lives of Moses, Abraham, Isaac, and Jacob, framed by some 40 ancient columns. Also compelling are the mosaics on the triumphal arch: the *Annunciation* and *Infancy of Christ*. In the 13th-century apse are mosaics by Jacopo Torriti, including the *Coronation of the Virgin* (1295), the pinnacle of Rome's medieval mosaic tradition. Look out, too, for mosaics in the entrance loggia by Filippo Rusuti. Other highlights include the Cappella Sistina (tomb of Pope Sixtus V) by Domenico Fontana, 1588; the Cappella Paolina, built by Paul V (1611); and Giovanni di Cosma's tomb of Cardinal Rodriguez (1299). The high altar reputedly contains relics of Christ's crib, the object of devotion of countless pilgrims.

HIGHLIGHTS

- Mosaics: upper tier of entrance loggia
- Coffered ceiling
- Mosaic cycle: 36 Old Testament scenes
- Mosaics: triumphal arch
- Apse mosaic: *Coronation of the Virgin*, Jacopo Torriti
- Four reliefs from a papal altar, Mino del Reame
- Fresco fragments: *Prophets*, attributed to Cimabue, Pietro Cavallini, or Giotto (apse)
- Cappella Sistina
- Cappella Paolina
- Tomb of Cardinal Rodriguez, Giovanni di Cosma

INFORMATION

- ✚ E6
- ✉ Piazza di Santa Maria Maggiore and Piazza dell'Esquilino
- ☎ 06 483 195
- 🕑 Apr–Sep: daily 7AM–8PM. Oct–Mar: daily 7–7
- Ⓜ Termini or Cavour
- 🚌 16, 27, 70, 71, 93, 93b to Piazza di Santa Maria Maggiore
- ♿ Poor: access is easiest from Piazza di Santa Maria Maggiore
- 💰 Free
- ↔ Palazzo Barberini (➤ 42), San Pietro in Vincoli (➤ 44)

SAN GIOVANNI IN LATERANO

HIGHLIGHTS

- Central portal: bronze doors
- Fresco: *Boniface VIII*, attributed to Giotto
- Cappella Corsini
- Frescoed tabernacle
- High altar reliquary
- Apse mosaic, Jacopo Torriti
- Cloister: columns and inlaid marble mosaics
- Papal altar: only the Pope can celebrate mass here
- Scala Santa
- Baptistery

INFORMATION

- F7
- Piazza di San Giovanni in Laterano
- 06 6988 6433, fax 06 6988 6452
- Church and cloister Apr–Sep: daily 7–7. Oct–Mar: 7–6. Scala Santa daily 6:15–12:15, 3–6:30. Baptistery summer: daily 9–1, 5–7. Winter: daily 9–1, 4–6
- San Giovanni
- 4, 15, 16, 85, 87, tram 13, 30b to Piazza di San Giovanni in Laterano
- Poor: steps to church
- Church, Scala Santa, Baptistery free. Cloister inexpensive
- Colosseum (► 43), San Pietro in Vincoli (► 44), San Clemente (► 46)

San Giovanni's facade can be seen from afar, its statues rising over the rooftops—a deliberate echo of St. Peter's—reminding us that this is the cathedral church of Rome and the Pope's titular see in his role as Bishop of Rome.

History A 4th-century palace here provided a meeting place for Pope Miltiades and Constantine (the first Christian emperor), later becoming a focus for Christianity. Barbarians, earthquakes, and fires destroyed the earliest churches on the site, so the facade, modeled on St. Peter's, dates from 1735, and Borromini's interior from 1646. It was the papal residence in Rome until the 14th century, when the popes moved to the Vatican, although pontiffs were crowned here until the 19th century.

Nave with statues of the Apostles

Interior Bronze doors from the Forum's Curia usher you into the cavernous interior, its chill whites and grays redeemed by a fabulously ornate ceiling. Other highlights include an apse mosaic by Jacopo Torriti (1288–94) and the beautiful cloister (off the north transept). A high altar reliquary is supposed to contain the heads of SS Peter and Paul, and a frescoed tabernacle is attributed to Arnolfo di Cambio and Fiorenzo de Lorenzo. Outside are the Scala Santa, reputedly the steps ascended by Christ at his trial in Jerusalem (the faithful climb up on their knees). The octagonal baptistery dates back to the time of Constantine and was the model for many subsequent baptisteries.

ROME's
best

49

ROMAN SITES

Triumphal arches

Two of Rome's greatest contributions to architecture were the basilica and the triumphal arch, the latter raised by the Roman Senate on behalf of a grateful populace to celebrate the achievements of victorious generals and emperors. Returning armies and their leaders would pass through the arches, bearing the spoils of war past a cheering crowd. Only three major arches survive in Rome—the arch of Constantine, and, in the Forum, the arches of Titus and Septimius Severus. But the influence of the form continues to be felt in London's Marble Arch and Paris's Arc de Triomphe.

ARCO DI COSTANTINO

Triumphal arches, like celebratory columns, were usually raised as monuments to military achievement, in this case the victory of Constantine over his rival Maxentius at the Ponte Milvio to the north of the city in AD 312. It was one of the last great monuments to be built in ancient Rome, and at 69 feet high and 85 feet wide it is also the largest and best-preserved of the city's arches. Most of its reliefs were taken from earlier buildings, partly out of pragmatism and partly out of a desire to link Constantine's glories with those of the past. The battle scenes of the central arch show Trajan at war with the Dacians, while another describes a boar hunt and sacrifice to Apollo, carved in the time of Hadrian (2nd century AD).

🔹 hIV; E6 ⊠ Piazza del Colosseo-Via di San Gregorio, Via dei Fori Imperiali 🕔 Always open 🚇 Colosseo 🚌 11, 13, 15, 27, 30b, 81, 85, 87, 118, 186, 673 to Piazza del Colosseo 💷 Free

BATHS OF CARACALLA

The Terme di Caracalla were not the largest baths in ancient Rome (those of Diocletian near the present-day Piazza della Repubblica were bigger). But they were the city's most luxurious, and could accommodate as many as 1,600 bathers at one time. Started by Septimius Severus in AD 206, and completed 11 years later by his son, Caracalla, they were designed as much as a gathering place as for hygiene, complete with gardens, libraries, sports facilities, stadiums, lecture rooms, shops—even hairdressers. They were open to both sexes, but bathing for men and women took place at different times. Something of the Terme's scale can still be gauged from today's ruins, although the site is perhaps now best known as the stage for outdoor opera in summer (► 81).

Carving from the Baths of Caracalla

🔹 E8 ⊠ Via delle Terme di Caracalla 52 ☎ 06 575 8626 🕔 Summer: Tue–Sat 9–1 hour before dusk. Sun, Mon 9–2. Winter: Tue–Sat 9–1 hour before dusk. Sun, Mon 9–1. Closed public hols 🚇 Circo Massimo 🚌 613, 671, 628, 714, 715 to Piazzale Numa Pompilio 💷 Moderate

CIRCO MASSIMO

This enormous grassy arena follows the outline of a stadium once capable of seating 300,000 people. Created to satisfy the passionate Roman appetite for chariot racing, and the prototype for almost all subsequent race courses, it was begun around 326 BC and modified frequently before the occasion of its last recorded use under Totila the Ostrogoth in AD 549. Much of the original structure was robbed of its stone—old monuments were often ransacked for building materials—but the *spina* (the circuit's dividing wall) remains, marked by a row of cypresses, the ruins of the imperial box, and the open arena, now a public park. Avoid after dark.

⊞ D7 ⊠ Via del Circo Massimo ☎ 06 780 1324
⊕ Always open Ⓜ Circo Massimo 🚌 11, 13, 15, 27, 30b, 94, 118, 673 to Piazza di Porta Capena 💷 Free

COLONNA DI MARCO AURELIO

The Column of Marcus Aurelius (AD 180–96) was built to celebrate Aurelius's military triumphs over hostile northern European tribes. It is composed of 27 separate drums of Carrara marble welded into a seamless whole, and is decorated with a continuous spiral of bas-reliefs commemorating episodes from the victorious campaigns. Aurelius is depicted no fewer than 59 times, though curiously never actually in battle. The summit statue is of St. Paul, and was crafted by Domenico Fontana in 1589 to replace the 60th depiction of Aurelius.

⊞ fII; D5 ⊠ Piazza Colonna, Via del Corso ⊕ Always open
Ⓜ Barberini 🚌 56, 60, 85, 119, 492 to Via del Corso 💷 Free

MERCATI TRAIANEI

Lack of space in the Roman Forum prompted the building of the new Imperial Fora (Fori Imperiali). They were begun in the 1st century BC by Julius Caesar and augmented by emperors Augustus, Vespasian, Nerva, and Trajan; the ruins of the buildings constructed during their rule lie either side of the Via dei Fori Imperiali. Part of the largest, Trajan's Forum, was the Mercati Traianei, constructed at the beginning of the 2nd century AD as a semicircular range of halls on three levels. Two survive in excellent condition, together with many of the 150 booths that once traded rare and expensive commodities; look in particular at the Via Biberata, named after *pipera* (pepper).

⊞ gIII; D6 ⊠ Via IV Novembre 94 ☎ 06 679 0048/06 6710 2802 ⊕ Apr–Sep: Tue–Sun 9–6. Oct–Mar: Tue–Sun 9–1 hour before dusk Ⓜ Cavour 🚌 57, 64, 65, 70, 75, 170 and other routes to Via IV Novembre 💷 Moderate

At the races

Going to the races was as much a social event in ancient times as it is today. All types of people attended meetings, but different classes were kept rigidly separated. The emperor and his entourage sat on the *pulvinar* (imperial balcony) while senators sat in the uppermost of the

Trajan's Forum

marble stalls. Lesser dignitaries occupied tiers of wooden seats, while the common rabble scrambled for standing room in open stands. The sexes, however, were unsegregated (unlike at the Colosseum), and the races became notorious for their sexual license. Ovid recorded that at the Circo there was "no call for the secret language of fingers: nor need you depend on a furtive nod when you set upon a new affair."

MUSEUMS

John Keats

It was in what is now the Museo Keats–Shelley that the young English poet John Keats died on February 23, 1821, aged just 25. He had arrived in Rome the previous September, sent south to seek a cure for consumption. He described his time in Rome, however, as a "posthumous life," lamenting that he "already seemed to feel the flowers growing over him." He was buried in the Protestant Cemetery (➤ 56). Percy Bysshe Shelley, a friend of Keats, came to live and write in Italy in 1818, but was drowned in the Bay of Spezia, near Livorno, four years later.

The Discus Thrower (Discobolus)

See Top 25 Sights for
CAPITOLINE MUSEUMS (➤ 37)
CASTEL SANT'ANGELO (➤ 27)
GALLERIA BORGHESE (➤ 45)
VATICAN MUSEUMS (➤ 25)
VILLA GIULIA (➤ 35)

MUSEO BARRACCO (PICCOLA FARNESINA)

This modest collection of Assyrian, Egyptian, Greek, Etruscan, and Roman artifacts is housed in the charming Piccola Farnesina, a miniature Renaissance palace.
➕ elII; C6 ✉ Corso Vittorio Emanuele II 158 ☎ 06 6880 6848 ⏰ Tue–Sat 9–7; Sun 9–1:30 🚌 46, 62, 64, 79, 81, 87, 186, 492, 926 to Corso Vittorio Emanuele II 🎫 Inexpensive (expensive for special exhibitions)

MUSEO KEATS–SHELLEY

Since 1909 this has been a museum and a library for students of the Romantic poets Keats and Shelley, both of whom died in Italy (see panel, left). Books, pamphlets, pictures, and essays lie scattered around the 18th-century house.
➕ gI; D5 ✉ Piazza di Spagna ☎ 06 678 4235 ⏰ Mon–Fri 9–1, 3–6 Ⓜ Spagna 🚌 119 to Piazza di Spagna 🎫 Moderate

MUSEO NAZIONALE ROMANO

One of the city's greatest museums. The cream of the collection, which includes a statue of a Gaul committing suicide and a throne depicting the birth of Aphrodite, is housed in two magnificent restored buildings. The Palazzo Massimo (1887) is filled with mosaics, wall paintings, and statues, including the *Discus Thrower*, a replica of the famous statue by Myron; and the Palazzo Altemps (*c*1480) contains a superb array of Classical busts and other sculpture.
Palazzo Massimo ➕ E5 ✉ Piazza dei Cinquecento 67 ☎ 06 4890 3500 ⏰ Tue–Sun 9–7 Ⓜ Repubblica 🚌 All services to Termini and Piazza dei Cinquecento 🎫 Expensive
Palazzo Altemps ➕ elI; C5 ✉ Piazza di Sant'Apollinare 44 ☎ 06 683 3759 ⏰ Tue–Sun 9–7 Ⓜ Spagna 🚌 70, 81, 87, 90, 186, 492 to Corso Rinascimento 🎫 Expensive

MUSEO DEL PALAZZO VENEZIA

Built in 1455 for Pietro Barbo (later Pope Paul II), and one of the city's first Renaissance palaces, the former Venetian Embassy became the property of the state in 1916; Mussolini harangued the crowds from the balconies. Today the museum hosts traveling exhibitions and a fine permanent collection that includes Renaissance paintings, sculpture, armor, ceramics, silverware, and objets d'art.
➕ fIII; D6 ✉ Palazzo Venezia, Via del Plebiscito 118 ☎ 06 679 8865/06 6999 4243 ⏰ Tue–Sat 9–1:30; Sun 9–12:30. Closed public hols 🚌 All services to Piazza Venezia 🎫 Expensive

ART GALLERIES

GALLERIA DELL'ACCADEMIA NAZIONALE DI SAN LUCA

An interesting collection of 18th- and 19th-century paintings, with earlier masterpieces by Raphael, Titian, Van Dyck, and Guido Reni.

➕ D5 ✉ Piazza dell'Accademia 77 ☎ 06 678 9243/06 679 8850 🕐 Mon, Wed, Fri, and last Sun of month 10–1 🚌 52, 53, 56, 58, 60, 61, 62, 71, 81, 95, 119 to Via del Tritone-Piazza Colonna 💵 Free

PALAZZO CORSINI

Though in a separate building, this gallery is part of the Palazzo Barberini's Galleria Nazionale. It houses later paintings from the national collection, with pictures by Rubens, Van Dyck, Murillo, and Caravaggio.

➕ dIV; C6 ✉ Via della Lungara 10 ☎ 06 6880 2323 🕐 Tue–Fri 9–7; Sat 9–2; Sun 9–1. Closed public hols 🚌 23, 65, 280 to Lungotevere Farnesina 💵 Moderate

PALAZZO SPADA

The pretty Palazzo Spada, with a creamy stucco facade (1556–60), contains four rooms of paintings by Guido Reni, Il Guercino, Michelangelo Cerquozzi, Albrecht Dürer, Andrea del Sarto, and others.

➕ eIII; C6 ✉ Piazza Capo di Ferro 3 ☎ 06 686 1158 🕐 Tue–Sat 9–7; Sun 9–1 🍴 Café 🚌 8, 44, 56, 60, 65, 75, 170, 181 to Via Arenula 💵 Expensive

PALAZZO-GALLERIA COLONNA

The best painting of this mostly 16th- to 18th-century (and rarely open) collection is Carracci's *Bean Eater*.

➕ gIII; D5 ✉ Via della Pilotta 17 ☎ 06 679 4362 🕐 Sep–Jul: Sat only 9–1. Closed Sun–Fri and Aug 🚌 57, 64, 65, 70, 75, 81, 170, and other buses to Piazza Venezia 💵 Moderate

VILLA FARNESINA

This lovely Renaissance villa was completed in 1511 for Agostino Chigi (see panel, right) by Baldassare Peruzzi, and later sold to the influential Farnese family. It is best known for the Loggia of Cupid and Psyche, decorated with frescoes (1517) by Raphael; for Il Sodoma's masterpiece, *Scenes from the Life of Alexander the Great*; and for the Salone delle Prospettive, Peruzzi's trompe l'oeil views of Rome.

➕ dIII; C6 ✉ Via della Lungara 230 ☎ 06 6880 1767 🕐 Tue–Sat 9–1 🚌 23, 65, 280 to Lungotevere Farnesina 💵 Moderate

A ceiling in the Villa Farnesina

Agostino Chigi

Agostino Chigi (*d*1512), from Siena, made his banking fortune by securing Rome's prize business —the papal account. He became renowned for flinging the family silver into the Tiber after gargantuan feasts at the Villa Farnesina. This extravagant gesture was not all it seemed, however, for Chigi omitted to tell his admiring diners that a net strung below the water caught the loot for the next banquet.

FOUNTAINS

Fontana delle Naiadi

Fontana delle Naiadi

The "Fountain of the Naiads" in Piazza della Repubblica, although of little historical interest or artistic value, is probably one of the most erotic works of art on public display anywhere in Italy. Designed by Mario Rutelli, the sculptures were added in 1901. Water plays seductively over four frolicking and suggestively clad bronze nymphs, each entwined in the phallic tentacles of one of four marine creatures. Each beast represents water in one of its forms: the swan signifying lakes, the sea-horse oceans, the water snake rivers, and the lizard underground streams.

**See Top 25 Sights for
FONTANA DI TREVI (▶ 39)**

FONTANA DELLE API

Bernini's small but captivating fountain was commissioned in honor of Pope Urban VIII, leading light of the Barberini clan. It depicts a scallop shell, a symbol of life and fertility—a favorite Bernini conceit—at which three bees (*api*), taken from the Barberini coat of arms, have settled to drink.
🞣 gI; E5 ✉ Piazza Barberini 🚇 Barberini 🚌 52, 53, 56, 58, 60, 95, 119, 492 to Piazza Barberini

FONTANA DELLA BARCACCIA

Commissioned by Pope Urban VIII, this eccentric little fountain (1627–29) at the base of the Spanish Steps (▶ 40) is the work of either Gian Lorenzo Bernini or his father Pietro. It represents a half-sunken ship and, translated literally, its name means Fountain of the Wretched Boat. Bernini was unable to create a greater aquatic display because of the low water pressure in the aqueduct feeding the fountain.
🞣 fI, D4–D5 ✉ Piazza di Spagna 🚇 Spagna 🚌 119 to Piazza di Spagna

FONTANA DEL MORO

Designed in 1575 by Giacomo della Porta, the fountain at Piazza Navona's southern end shows a North African "Moor" (actually a marine divinity) grappling with a dolphin, a figure added by Antonio Mori from a design by Bernini.
🞣 elI; C5 ✉ Piazza Navona 🚌 70, 81, 87, 90, 186, 492 to Corso del Rinascimento, or 46, 62, 64 to Corso Vittorio Emanuele II

FONTANA PAOLA

The five arches and six granite columns of the monumental facade fronting this majestic fountain were built between 1610 and 1612 to carry the waters of Trajan's aqueduct, which had been restored by Pope Paul V. The columns were removed from the old St. Peter's, while many of the precious marbles were filched from the Temple of Minerva in the Imperial Fora.
🞣 cIV; C6–C7 ✉ Via Garibaldi 🚌 41, 144 to the Gianicolo

FONTANA DEI QUATTRO FIUMI

Bernini's spirited Fountain of the Four Rivers at the heart of Piazza Navona was designed for Pope Innocent X in 1648 as part of a scheme to improve the approach to the Palazzo Doria Pamphili. It was unveiled in 1651. Its four figures represent the four rivers of Paradise (the Nile, Ganges, Danube, and Plate), and the four "corners" of the world (Africa, Asia, Europe, and America). The dove atop the central obelisk is a symbol of the Pamphili family, of which Innocent was a member.

✚ ell; C5 ✉ Piazza Navona 🚌 70, 81, 87, 90, 186, 492 to Corso del Rinascimento, or 46, 62, 64 to Corso Vittorio Emanuele II

FONTANA DELLE TARTARUGHE
This tiny creation (1581–4) is one of Rome's most delightful sights, thanks to the tortoises, probably added by Bernini in 1658 (they are now copies).

✚ flll; D6 ✉ Piazza Mattei 🚌 44, 56, 60, 65, 75, 170, 181, 710, 718, 719 to Via Arenula

FONTANA DEL TRITONE
Like its companion piece, the Fontana delle Api (► 54), the Fountain of Triton (1643) was also designed by Bernini for Urban VIII. One of the sculptor's earliest fountains, the Fontana del Tritone is made of travertine rather than the more usual marble. It depicts four dolphins supporting twin scallop shells bearing the Barberini coat of arms, on which the triumphant Triton is enthroned.

✚ gl; E5 ✉ Piazza Barberini 🚇 Barberini 🚌 52, 53, 56, 58, 60, 95, 119, 492 to Piazza Barberini

LE QUATTRO FONTANE
These four linked fountains (1588–93) sit at a busy crossroads close to Via Nazionale. Each contains a reclining deity: the two female figures are probably Juno and Diana; the male figure is the Nile or Aniene; and the last figure, shown with the she-wolf, is a river god representing the Tiber.

✚ hll; E5 ✉ Via delle Quattro Fontane-Via del Quirinale 🚇 Repubblica 🚌 57, 64, 65, 70, 75, 81, 170 to Via Nazionale

Artistic rivalry
Well-worn Roman myths surround Bernini's Fontana dei Quattro Fiumi. One suggests the veiled figure of the Nile symbolizes the sculptor's dislike for the church of Sant'Agnese, designed by his fierce rival, Borromini (the veil actually symbolizes the river's unknown source). Another claims the figure representing the Plate is holding up his arm as if in horror of the church (either appalled by its design or afraid it is about to fall down). However, neither theory is correct, for Bernini finished the fountain before Borromini had even begun work on his church.

Fontana dei Quattro Fiumi

PARKS & GARDENS

The Protestant Cemetery

"...the cypress trees cast their long shadows upon the most extraordinary collection of exiles ever assembled in one place."
H. V. Morton,
A Traveller in Rome.

"The Cemetery is an open space among the ruins, covered in winter with violets and daisies. It might make one in love with death to know that one should be buried in so sweet a place."
Percy Bysshe Shelley,
Preface to *Adonis.*

Via Appia Antica

CIMITERO PROTESTANTE
Described on more than one occasion as the "most beautiful cemetery in the world," the bucolic Protestant Cemetery is also something of a literary shrine (see panel, left), owing to the graves of poets such as the young Englishman John Keats, whose tombstone bears the epitaph "Here lies One whose Name was Writ in Water." As late as the 19th century, burials here had to take place at night to avoid provoking attacks from outraged Catholics.
✚ D8 ⊠ Via Caio Cestio 6, Testaccio ☎ 06 574 1141/1900
🕐 Tue–Sun 9–2 hours before dusk, but subject to change without notice
🚌 13, 23, 27, 30b, 57, 94, 95, 716 to Piazza di Porta San Paolo
💰 Free but donation expected

ORTO BOTANICO
Trastevere has few open spaces, so these university gardens and their 7,000 or so botanical species—originally part of the Palazzo Corsini—provide a welcome slice of green shade.
✚ cIV; C6 ⊠ Largo Cristina di Svezia, off Via Corsini ☎ 06 686 4193 🕐 Summer: Mon–Sat 9–6:30. Winter: Mon–Sat 9–5:30. Closed public hols 🚌 23, 65, 280 to Lungotevere Farnesina 💰 Inexpensive

PALATINO E ORTI FARNESIANI
After a stroll around the Forum it's worth making time to climb the Palatine Hill to enjoy this haven, designed in the 16th century by the great Renaissance architect Giacomo Vignola. Orange groves, cypresses, and endless drowsy corners, all speckled with flowers and ancient stones, make up the Orti Farnesiani, which were laid out over the ruins of the palace that once stood here.
✚ gIV; D6 ⊠ Entrances from Via di San Gregorio and for the Roman Forum at Largo Romolo e Remo on Via dei Fori Imperiali ☎ 06 699 0110 🕐 Tue–Sat 9–1 hour before dusk; Sun, Mon 9–2 🚇 Colosseo
🚌 11, 27, 81, 85, 87, 186 to Via dei Fori Imperiali 💰 Expensive

PARCO OPPIO
This homey area of park, once part of a palace complex built by Nero and redeveloped by Trajan, rests the eyes and feet after visits to the Colosseum, San Clemente or San Giovanni in Laterano. A community meeting place, it's a welcoming mixture of grass and walkways (and feral cats), complete with promenading mothers, a small café, and a children's playground.
✚ hIV; E6 ⊠ Via Labicana-Viale del Monte Oppio 🕐 Always open
🚌 11, 15, 16, 27, 81, 85 to Via Labicana 💰 Free

PARCO SAVELLO
Close to Santa Sabina (a pretty church in its own right), the little-known Parco Savello lies closer to the center than you might expect. Its hilly position

provides a lovely panorama over the Tiber and the city beyond.
🟥 D7 ✉ Via Santa Sabina, Aventino ⏰ Daily dawn–dusk 🚌 94 👣 Free

PINCIO

The park was laid out in the early 19th century, but the hill site has always been popular: in ancient times the patricians built lavish

Villa Doria Pamphili

villas and gardens here. Even if you cannot face the longer trip to the nearby Villa Borghese, be sure to walk to the Pincio from Piazza del Popolo or Piazza di Spagna to enjoy the wonderful views (best at dusk) across the rooftops to St. Peter's.
🟥 D4 ✉ Piazza del Pincio ⏰ Daily dawn–dusk 🚌 90, 90b, 95, 119, 926 to Piazzale Flaminio or Piazza del Popolo 👣 Free

VIA APPIA ANTICA

Once an imperial highway, this old roadway so close to the city center is now an evocative cobbled lane fringed with ancient monuments, tombs, catacombs, and lovely open country (see panel).
🟥 F9 ✉ Via Appia Antica ⏰ Always open 🚌 118 from the Colosseum, San Giovanni in Laterano, or the Baths of Caracalla 👣 Free

VILLA BORGHESE

Rome's largest central park was laid out between 1613 and 1616 as the grounds of the Borghese family's summer villa. Smaller now, and redesigned in the 18th century during the fashion for informal, English-style parks, it still offers a shady retreat. Walkways, woods, and lakes are complemented by fountains, a racetrack, and children's playgrounds. There is also a zoo, although it is rather tawdry.
🟥 D4–E4 ✉ Porta Pinciana-Via Flaminia ⏰ Daily dawn–dusk Ⓜ Flaminio 🚌 3, 4, 52, 53, 57, 95, 490, 495, 910 👣 Free

VILLA CELIMONTANA

Set on one of the southern hills of ancient Rome and scattered with the remains of ancient buildings, this is one of Rome's lesser-known parks, easily accessible from the Colosseum and San Giovanni in Laterano.
🟥 E7 ✉ Piazza della Navicella ⏰ Daily 7–dusk 🚌 81, 673 to Via Claudia 👣 Free

VILLA DORIA PAMPHILI

This huge area of parkland—laid out for Prince Camillo Pamphili in the mid-17th century—is probably too far from the center if you are just making a short visit to Rome. If you have time to spare, however, and fancy a good long walk away from the hordes, there is nowhere better.
🟥 A7 ✉ Via di San Pancrazio ⏰ Daily dawn–dusk 🚌 41, 144 to the Gianicolo 👣 Free

Via Appia Antica

The Appian Way was built in 312 BC by Appius Claudius Caecus to link Rome with Capua; in 194 BC it was extended to Brindisi (320 miles and 13 days' march away). In 71 BC it was the spot where 6,000 of Spartacus's troops were crucified during a slaves' revolt; it bore witness to the funeral processions of Sulla (78 BC) and Augustus (AD 14); it was the road along which St. Paul was marched as prisoner in AD 56; and close to the city walls was the point at which St. Peter (fleeing Rome) encountered Christ and, famously, asked him *"Domine, quo vadis?"* ("Lord, where are you going?").

MOSAICS

See Top 25 Sights for
SAN CLEMENTE (➤ 46)
SAN GIOVANNI IN LATERANO (➤ 48)
SANTA MARIA MAGGIORE (➤ 47)
SANTA MARIA IN TRASTEVERE (➤ 28)

Mosaics

Mosaics were a major decorative feature of ancient Roman buildings and later Christian churches. Wall paintings were equally popular, but less resilient, which is why so few survive from the Roman period. Some of the best wall decorations of the Classical age can be seen in the Palazzo Massimo (➤ 52). Many

Santa Prassede ceiling mosaics

Roman techniques and traditions were inherited from the Greeks, and over the centuries tastes varied between monochrome backgrounds and simple pattern mosaics to highly colored and detailed narratives. Christian mosaics in churches initially copied Roman and Greek models, but increasingly adopted the brilliant gold backgrounds used in Byzantine mosaics from the east.

SANT'AGNESE FUORI LE MURA

Compare the outstanding Byzantine 7th-century mosaics in the apse of Sant'Agnese Fuori le Mura (St. Agnes Outside the Walls) with the earlier mosaics in Santa Costanza. The church was built around AD 342 by Constantia to be close to the tomb of the martyred Sant'Agnese. Although clumsily restored in 1855, the mosaics have survived intact. They show Agnes, with the sword of her martyrdom at her feet, flanked by the church's 7th-century rebuilder Pope Honorius I.

G3 · Via Nomentana 349 · 06 861 0840 · Daily 8–noon, 4–7:30 · 36, 36b, 37, 60, 62, 136, 137 to Via Nomentana-Via di Santa Costanza · Free

SANTA COSTANZA

Exquisite 4th-century mosaics stand out in this church, originally built as a mausoleum for Constantia and Helena, Emperor Constantine's daughters. Note their white background, in contrast to the gold in later Byzantine work, and the pagan icons adapted to Christian use—especially the lamb and peacock, symbols of innocence and immortality respectively.

G3 · Via Nomentana 349 · 06 861 0840 · Mon 9–noon; Tue–Sat 9–noon, 4–6; Sun noon–6 · 36, 36b, 37, 60, 62, 136, 137 to Via Nomentana-Via di Santa Costanza · Inexpensive

SANTA MARIA IN DOMNICA AND SANTO STEFANO ROTONDO

Like those in Santa Prassede (➤ 59), the glorious mosaics in the apse of the 9th-century Santa Maria in Domnica were commissioned by Pope Paschal I, depicted at the foot of the Virgin and Child (his square halo indicates he was alive when the mosaic was created). Almost opposite this church is Santo Stefano Rotondo, with a 7th-century mosaic commemorating two martyrs buried nearby, and some gruesome frescoes depicting torture.

Santa Maria · E7 · Piazza della Navicella 12 · 06 700 1519 · Daily 8:30–noon, 3:30–6 · 81, 673 to Via della Navicella · Free

Santo Stefano · E7 · 06 7049 3717 · Oct–Mar: Mon 2–4:30; Tue–Sat 9–1, 2–4:30. May–Jun, Sep: Mon–Sat 9–1, 3:30–6. Jul–Aug: Tue–Sat 9–12:30 · 81, 673 to Via della Navicella · Free

SANTA PRASSEDE

The treasure of this church is its stunning, gold-encrusted mosaic commissioned by Pope Paschal I in 822 for his mother's mausoleum in the Cappella di San Zeno. So beautiful were the mosaics that in the Middle Ages the chapel became known as the Garden of Paradise. Similar Byzantine mosaics adorn the church's apse and triumphal arch.

🚇 E6 ✉ Via Santa Prassede 9a ☎ 06 488 2456 🕐 Daily 7:30–noon, 4–6:30 🚌 11, 27 to Via Cavour-Piazza Esquilino 💶 Free

SANTA PUDENZIANA

Built in the 4th century but much altered over the years, this church was reputedly raised over the house of the Roman senator Pudens, site of St. Peter's conversion of the senator's daughters, Pudenziana and Prassede. Its prized apse mosaic dates from this period, an early Christian depiction of a golden-robed Christ, the Apostles, and two women presumed to be Prassede and Pudenziana.

🚇 hII; E5 ✉ Via Urbana 160 ☎ 06 481 4622 🕐 Apr–Sep: daily 8–noon, 3–6. Oct–Mar: daily 3–6 🚇 Termini 🚌 70, 71 to Via A de Pretis, or 11, 27 to Via Cavour-Piazza Esquilino 💶 Free

SANTI COSMA E DAMIANO

This church is part of the former Forum of Vespasian, one of the Imperial Fora, although a 1632 rebuilding wiped out all but a few vestiges of its original classical and medieval splendor. Chief among the surviving treasures is the 6th-century Byzantine mosaic in the apse, *The Second Coming*, a work whose mastery of color and pattern influenced Roman and other mosaicists for centuries to come.

🚇 gIV; D6 ✉ Via dei Fori Imperiali ☎ 06 699 1540 🕐 Daily 8–1, 4–7 🚌 All routes to Piazza Venezia and 11, 27, 81, 85, 87, 186 to Via Fori Imperiali 💶 Free

Mosaics in Cappella di San Zeno, Santa Prassede

Sant'Agnese (St. Agnes)

St. Agnes, who was martyred in Piazza Navona and buried near Sant'Agnese, was one of the most popular early Christian martyrs—despite the recorded fact that she failed to take a bath in the 13 years she was alive (such was her modesty). According to legend, this beautiful girl was martyred for refusing to marry the son of a pagan governor of the city. As an earlier punishment she was thrown into a brothel, but as she was about to be paraded naked her hair grew miraculously to spare her blushes. St. Agnes' steadfastness made her a symbol of Christian chastity, and her tomb became a place of pilgrimage particularly venerated by Roman women.

Mosaics in Santa Prassede

59

CHURCHES

SANTA MARIA DELLA CONCEZIONE

Rome's most ghoulish sight lurks behind an unassuming facade in the unlikely surroundings of

Santa Maria in Cosmedin

the Via Vittorio Veneto. Lying in the crypt of Santa Maria della Concezione are the remains of 4,000 Capuchin monks, some still dressed in jaunty clothes, the bones of others crafted into macabre chandeliers and bizarre wall decorations. The bodies were originally buried in soil especially imported from Jerusalem. When this ran out they were left uncovered, a practice that continued until 1870. The church was built in 1624 by Cardinal Antonio Barberini, brother of Urban VIII, a Capuchin friar who lies buried before the main altar under a cheerful legend: *"hic jacet pulvis cinis et nihil"* ("here lie dust, ashes, and nothing"). The church is known for Guido Reni's painting *St. Michael Trampling the Devil*, in which the Devil is reputedly a portrait of the Pamphili Pope Innocent X.

➕ gI; E5 ✉ Via Vittorio Veneto 27 ☎ 06 487 1185 🔵 Church daily 7–noon, 4–7. Crypt (Cimitero dei Cappuccini) daily 9–noon, 3–6 🚌 52, 53, 56, 58, 58b, 95, 490, 495, and others to Via Vittorio Veneto 💲 Free (donation to visit crypt)

La Bocca della Verità

The "Mouth of Truth" is a gaping marble mouth set in a stone face. Anyone suspected of lying—particularly a woman accused of adultery—would have his or her right hand forced into the maw. Legend claims that in the case of dissemblers the mouth would clamp shut and sever their fingers. To give credence to the story a priest supposedly hid behind the stone to hit the fingers of those known to be guilty.

SANTA MARIA IN COSMEDIN

This lovely old medieval church—one of the most atmospheric in the city—is best known for the Bocca della Verità, a weatherbeaten stone face (of the sea god Oceanus) once used by the ancient Romans as a drain cover. Inside, the church has a beautiful floor, twin pulpits, a bishop's throne, and a stone choir screen, all decorated in fine Cosmati stone inlay. Most date from the 12th century, a little earlier than the impressive *baldacchino* (altar canopy), which was built by Deodato di Cosma in 1294. Tucked away in a small room off the right aisle is the mosaic *Adoration of the Magi*, almost all that remains of an 8th-century Greek church on the site.

➕ D7 ✉ Piazza Bocca della Verità ☎ 06 678 1419 🔵 Daily 9–noon, 3–5 🚌 15, 23, 57, 94, 95, 160, 716 to Piazza Bocca della Verità 💲 Free

ROME
where to...

EXPENSIVE RESTAURANTS

Prices

Approximate price per person for a meal, including wine:

Expensive	L100,000 or more
Mid-range	L60,000–100,000
Budget	L60,000 or less

The menu

Starters are called antipasti; first course (soup, pasta, or risotto) is *il primo*; and main meat and fish dishes are *il secondo*. Salads (*insalata*) and vegetables (*contorni*) are ordered (and often eaten) separately. Desserts are *dolci*, with cheese (*formaggio*) or fruit (*frutta*) to follow. If no menu card is offered, ask for *la lista* or *il menù*. A set-price menu (*un menù turistico*) may seem good value, but portions are small and the food is invariably poor— usually just spaghetti with a tomato sauce, followed by a piece of chicken and fruit.

Change of career

According to a legend, La Rosetta's famous owner, the Sicilian Carmelo Riccioli, abandoned a career as a boxer and a sports writer when he won this restaurant as payment for a bet.

ALBERTO CIARLA

Among Rome's best fish restaurants, with a fine wine list. The food is elegantly presented, the candlelight lovely, and the service impeccable.
➕ C7 ✉ Piazza San Cosimato 40 ☎ 06 581 8668 🕓 Closed Sun and daily at lunch. Closed two weeks in Aug and Jan 🚌 44, 75, 170, 181, 280, 717 to Viale di Trastevere

CHECCHINO DAL 1887

Robust appetites are required for this menu. Quintessential Roman dishes relying largely on offal are the specialty. Booking recommended.
➕ C8–D8 ✉ Via Monte Testaccio 30 ☎ 06 574 6318 🕓 Tue–Sat 12:30–3, 8:30–11. Closed Aug 🚌 13, 23, 27, 57, 95, 716 to Piramide and Via Marmorata

EL TOULÀ

Considered by many to be Rome's best restaurant, with a mixture of Venetian and international cuisine. Service is formal—in keeping with the traditional atmosphere.
➕ el; D5 ✉ Via della Lupa 29b ☎ 06 687 3498 🕓 Mon–Fri 1–3, 8–11; Sat 8–11PM. Closed Aug 🚌 81, 90 to Via del Corso-Largo Carlo Goldini

IL CONVIVIO

The Troiani brothers from Italy's Marche region have created a tranquil little restaurant with a reputation for innovative and subtly flavored modern dishes.
➕ ell; C5 ✉ Via dell'Orso 44 ☎ 06 686 9432 🕓 Mon–Sat

1–2:30, 8–10:30. Closed May 🚌 70, 81, 90, 90b, 186 to Ponte Umberto-Lungotevere Marzio

LA ROSETTA

An exclusive fish and seafood restaurant whose popularity means booking is a must.
➕ ell; D5 ✉ Via della Rosetta 8–9 ☎ 06 686 1002 🕓 Mon–Fri 1–3, 8–11:30; Sat 8–11:30. Closed 3 weeks in Aug 🚌 119 to Piazza della Rotonda, or 70, 81, 87, 90 to Corso del Rinascimento

SABATINI

Once Rome's most famous restaurant, Sabatini is still favored for its reliable food and lovely setting, though prices are higher than the cooking deserves. Reservations essential.
➕ dlV; C6 ✉ Piazza Santa Maria in Trastevere 13 ☎ 06 581 2026 ➕ dlV, C6 ✉ Vicolo Santa Maria in Trastevere 18 ☎ 06 581 8307 🕓 Mon, Tue, Thu–Sun noon–2:30; 7:30–11. Closed Wed, Aug 🚌 44, 56, 60, 75, 170, 181, 280 to Piazza Sidney Sonnino

VECCHIA ROMA

In a pretty piazza and perfect for an alfresco meal on a summer evening. Although the 18th-century interior is also captivating, prices are high for what is only straightforward and reliable Roman cooking.
➕ flV; D6 ✉ Piazza Campitelli 18 ☎ 06 686 4604 🕓 Mon, Tue, Thu–Sun 1–3, 8–11 🚌 44, 46, 56, 60, 75, 85, 87, 94 and all other services to Piazza Venezia

MID-RANGE RESTAURANTS

AL 34
Roman and southern Italian cooking, and a romantic, candlelit intimacy. Close to Via Condotti and the Spanish Steps. Reserve ahead.
🔹 fI; D5 ✉ Via Mario de' Fiori 34 ☎ 06 679 5091 🕐 Tue–Sun 12:30–3, 7:30–11. Closed 3 weeks in Aug 🚇 Spagna 🚌 119

SORA LELLA
Founded by the legendary actress and cook Sora Lella, and now presided over by her son and nephews, this is a two-room, wood-paneled former trattoria on the Isola Tiberina. Roman cooking, with menu and daily specials posted on a board.
🔹 fIV; D6 ✉ Via Ponte Quattro Capi ☎ 06 686 1601 🕐 Mon–Sat 12:30–2;30, 7:30–10.30. Closed Aug 🚌 23, 717, 774, 780

IL BACARO
Tiny but gracious restaurant north of the Pantheon; can be noisy, but the light, modern pan-Italian cooking is excellent.
🔹 eII; D5 ✉ Via degli Spagnoli 27, near Piazza delle Coppelle ☎ 06 686 4110 🕐 Mon–Sat 8AM–11:30PM. Closed Aug 🚇 Spagna 🚌 119

NERONE
A small, friendly, old-fashioned trattoria just a few steps north of the Colosseum that is best known for its antipasti buffet and simple Abruzzese cooking. Has a handful of outside tables.
🔹 hIV; E6 ✉ Via delle Terme di Tito 96 ☎ 06 474 5207

🕐 Mon–Sat noon–3, 7–11. Closed Aug 🚌 11, 13, 27, 30, 81, 85, 87, 186 to Piazza del Colosseo

PAPÀ GIOVANNI
Currently among the city's better restaurants, with light and often innovative cooking—and prices higher than they are at some other mid-price choices. Located off Corso del Rinascimento.
🔹 eIII; C5 ✉ Via dei Sediari 4 ☎ 06 686 5308 🕐 Mon–Sat 1–3, 8–11. Closed Aug 🚌 70, 81, 87 to Corso del Rinascimento

PARIS
An extremely popular and elegant little restaurant just south of Piazza Santa Maria in Trastevere, and known for its fish, pastas, and Roman cuisine. Outside tables for alfresco dining. Reservations essential.
🔹 dIV; C7 ✉ Piazza San Callisto 7a ☎ 06 581 5378 🕐 Tue–Sat 12:30–3, 8–11; Sun 12:30–3. Closed 3 weeks in Aug 🚌 8, 44, 56, 60, 75, 170, 181, 280, 717 to Piazza Sidney Sonnino

ROMOLO
A long-established fixture in Trastevere, housed in what was reputedly the home of Raphael's model and mistress, the "Fornarina" (baker's daughter). An outside courtyard is candlelit for dinner.
🔹 dIV; C7 ✉ Via Porta Settimiana 8 ☎ 06 581 8284 🕐 Tue–Sun 12:30–2:30, 7:30–11:30. Closed 3 weeks in Aug 🚌 23, 65, 280 to Lungotevere Farnesina

Roman specialties
Roman favorites— though they are by no means confined to the city— include pastas like *bucatini all'Amatriciana* (tomato sauce, salt pork, and chili peppers); *spaghetti alla carbonara* (egg, bacon, pepper, and cheese); and *gnocchi alla Romana* (small potato or semolina dumplings with tomato or butter). The best-known main course is *saltimbocca alla Romana* (veal scallops with ham and sage, cooked in wine and butter). Also traditional are *trippa* (tripe), *cervelli* (brains), and *coda alla vaccinara* (oxtail).

BUDGET RESTAURANTS

Restaurant etiquette

Italians have a strongly developed sense of how to behave, which applies in restaurants as much as anywhere else. It is considered bad form to order only one course in any restaurant—if that is what you want, go to a pizzeria. The concept of a doggie-bag could not be more at odds with Italian ideas of eating out. You might succeed in getting a doggie bag if you want one, but you will pay a very high price in the loss of your dignity.

AUGUSTO

One of Trastevere's last remaining inexpensive and authentic family-run trattorias, with 50 places. No credit cards.

📍 dIV; C6 ✉ Piazza de' Renzi 15 ☎ 06 580 3798
🕐 Mon–Fri 1–3:30, 8–11. Closed Aug 🚌 23, 65, 280 to Lungotevere Sanzio, or 44, 56, 60, 75, 170 to Piazza Sidney Sonnino

BIRRERIA FRATELLI TEMPERA

Ideal for a simple lunch or dinner. Original art nouveau interior and a large and easy-going beer hall. Especially busy at lunchtimes.

📍 fll; D5 ✉ Via di San Marcello 19 ☎ 06 678 6203
🕐 Mon–Sat 12:30–2:45, 7:30–11 🚌 44, 46, 64, 75, 85, 87, 94 and all other buses to Piazza Venezia

DAL TOSCANO

Large trattoria with Tuscan food convenient for St. Peter's: particularly known for its meats (including classic *bistecca alla fiorentina*) and its wood-fired grill. Service can be hurried.

📍 B4 ✉ Via Germanico 58 ☎ 06 63972 5717 🕐 Tue–Sun 12:30–2:30, 7:30–11. Closed Mon, Aug and 2 weeks in Dec
🚇 Ottaviano 🚌 23, 32, 34, 81

DA VALENTINO

A tiny, old-fashioned trattoria close to the Forum.

📍 hlll; E6 ✉ Via Cavour 293 ☎ 06 488 1303 🕐 Mon–Thu, Sat, Sun noon–3, 7–10
🚇 Cavour 🚌 11, 27, 81 to Via Cavour, or 85, 87, 186 to Via dei Fori Imperiali

FIASCHETTERIE BELTRAMME DA CESARETTO

In a historical monument, with a fine courtyard outside. Inside, shared tables keep things convivial. Convenient to the Spanish Steps.

📍 fI; D5 ✉ Via della Croce 39 🕐 Mon–Sat 12:15–3, 7:30–11. Closed 2 weeks in Aug 🚇 Spagna
🚌 119 to Piazza di Spagna, or 81, 90 to Via del Corso

FILETTI DI BACCALÀ

At this tiny place with Formica tables, you wash down cod with plenty of beer or crisp local wine. Close to Campo de' Fiori.

📍 elll; C6 ✉ Largo dei Librari 88, off Via dei Giubbonari 🕐 Mon–Sat 12:30–2:30, 7–10:30 🚌 44, 56, 60, 65, 75, 170, 181, 710, 718, 719 to Via Arenula

GRAPPOLO D'ORO

This unspoilt trattoria has been a favorite with locals and foreign residents for decades. Menu features *pasta all'amatriciana* and *scaloppine* any way you like.

📍 elll; C6 ✉ Piazza della Cancelleria 80 ☎ 06 689 7080 🕐 Mon–Sat 12:30–2:30, 7:30–10:30 🚌 46, 62, 64 to Corso Vittorio Emanuele II

ORSO 80

Big, lively and often busy with tourists, but standards remain high. Known for its antipasti buffet, also meat, fish, and seafood.

📍 ell; C5 ✉ Via dell'Orso 33 ☎ 06 686 4904 🕐 Tue–Sun 12:30–2:30, 7:15–10:30. Closed Mon and Aug 🚌 70, 87, 186 to Via Monte Brianzo or 70, 81, 87, 186 to Corso della Rinascimento

PIZZERIAS

BAFFETTO ($)

Rome's most famous pizzeria. A tiny, hole-in-the wall classic that has retained its atmosphere and low prices despite its fame. Expect lines.

dII; C5 Via del Governo Vecchio 114, corner of Via Sora 06 686 1617 Mon–Sat 6:30PM–12:45AM 46, 62, 64 to Corso Vittorio Emanuele II

CORALLO ($)

This stylish pizzeria is convenient to Piazza Navona. Full meals also available.

dII; C5 Via del Corallo 10, off Via del Governo Vecchio 06 6830 7703 Tue–Sun 7:30PM–1:30AM. Closed 1 week in Aug 46, 62, 64 to Corso Vittorio Emanuele II

DA VITTORIO ($)

Tiny Neapolitan-run Trastevere pizzeria that makes a good standby if Ivo (see below) is busy.

C7 Via di San Cosimato 14a, off Piazza San Callisto 06 580 0353 Mon–Sat 7PM–midnight 8, 44, 56, 60, 75, 170, 181, 280, 717 to Viale di Trastevere

EST! EST! EST! ($)

Among Rome's oldest pizzerias; worth the slight walk if you are near Stazione Termini.

hII; E5 Via Genova 32 06 488 1107 Tue–Sun 6:30–11:30PM. Closed Aug Repubblica 57, 64, 65, 70, 71, 75, 170 to Via Nazionale

IVO ($)

The best-known of Trastevere's pizzerias. Lines are common but turnover is quick.

C7 Via di San Francesco a Ripa 158 06 581 7082 Wed–Mon 5:30–2AM. Closed 3 weeks in Aug 8, 44, 56, 60, 75, 170, 181, 280, 717 to Viale di Trastevere

LA CAPRICCIOSA ($)

Roomy and rather stylish, with a terrace for alfresco eating. Reputedly the birthplace of the *capricciosa* pizza (ham, egg, artichoke, and olives). Full meals also served; pizzas available evenings only.

fI; D5 Largo dei Lombardi 8, Via del Corso 06 687 8480 Mon, Wed–Sun 12:15AM–3PM, 7PM–12:30AM. Closed 3 weeks in Aug Spagna 81, 90, 119 to Via del Corso-Via della Croce

LEONCINO ($)

Nothing has changed in the wonderful old-fashioned interior for over 30 years. The retro feel has made it popular, so expect a line. Open for lunch.

fI; D5 Via del Leoncino 28, Piazza San Lorenzo in Lucina 06 687 6306 Mon–Tue, Thu–Fri 1–2:30PM, 7PM–midnight ; Sat 7PM–midnight Spagna 81, 90, 119 to Via del Corso-Via Tomacelli

PANATTONI ($)

Big, bright, and often busy, Panattoni is known locally as "L'Obitorio" (The Morgue) on account of its cold marble tables. Seating also outside on Viale di Trastevere.

eIV; C7 Viale di Trastevere 53 06 580 0919 Thu–Tue 6:30PM–2AM. Closed 3 weeks in Aug 44, 56, 60, 75, 170, 181, 280, 717 to Viale di Trastevere

Prices

Where appropriate, an indication of the cost of an establishment is given by $ signs:

$$$ denotes higher prices,

$$ denotes average prices,

$ denotes lower prices.

The check

The check, *il conto*, usually includes extras such as *servizio* (service). Iniquitous cover charges (*pane e coperto*) have recently been outlawed, but some restaurants still try to get round the new regulations. Only pay for bread (*pane*) if you have asked for it. Proper checks—not a scrawled piece of paper—must be given by law. If you receive a scrap of paper—it's more likely in a pizzeria—and have doubts about the total, be sure to ask for a proper receipt (*una fattura* or *una ricevuta*).

ETHNIC & INTERNATIONAL RESTAURANTS

Unusual waitresses

You are served at the L'Eau Vive by nuns from a third world order known as the Vergini Laiche Cristiane di Azione Cattolica Missionaria per Mezzo del Lavoro (Christian Virgins of Catholic Missionary Action though Work). With restaurants in several parts of the world, their aim is to spread the message of Christianity through the medium of French food. To this end, dining is interrupted by prayers each evening at 9.

AFRICA ($)

A long-established restaurant close to Termini, catering mainly to Rome's Ethiopian and Eritrean population with dishes such as *injera* (pancakes served with meat).

➕ F5 ✉ Via Gaeta 26 ☎ 06 494 1077 🕐 Tue–Sun 9AM–1PM. Closed 2 weeks in Aug 🚌 38, 57, 319 to Via Volturno and all buses to Termini

BIRRERIA VIENNESE ($)

An authentic beer house with a wide range of Austro-German specialties.

➕ fI; D5 ✉ Via della Croce 21 ☎ 06 679 5569 🕐 Daily Ⓜ Spagna 🚌 81, 90 to Via del Corso, or 119 to Piazza di Spagna

CHARLY'S SAUCIÈRE ($$)

Cozy and established, offering reliable French and Swiss staples (40 places).

➕ hIV; F7 ✉ Via di San Giovanni in Laterano 270 ☎ 06 7049 5666 🕐 Mon–Sat 8PM–midnight. Closed 2 weeks in Aug 🚌 85 to Via San Giovanni in Laterano

GEORGE'S ($$$)

One of the city's leading restaurants, established over 50 years ago, although the splendor of its *dolce vita* heyday is now slightly faded. The French, Italian, and international cuisine is good, but rarely exceptional. Polished service: jacket, tie, and reservations essential.

➕ E4 ✉ Via Marche 7 ☎ 06 4208 4575 🕐 Mon–Sat 12:30–3, 7:30PM–1AM. Closed Aug Ⓜ Spagna 🚌 52, 53, 56, 58, 95 to Via Vittorio Veneto

GIGGETTO ($)

A famous Romano-Jewish restaurant in the Ghetto district, it's almost as good and slightly cheaper than Piperno.

➕ fIV; D6 ✉ Via Portico d'Ottavia 21a ☎ 06 686 1105 🕐 Tue–Sun 12:30–2:30, 7:30–10:30 🚌 8, 44, 56, 60, 65, 75, 170, 181, 710, 718, 719 to Via Arenula

L'EAU VIVE ($$–$$$)

A pleasantly bizarre dining experience. The predominantly French food is served by nuns (see panel). Politicians, celebrities, and locals alike come to enjoy the food and the beautiful 16th-century frescoed dining rooms.

➕ eIII; D6 ✉ Via Monterone 85 ☎ 06 654 1095 or 06 6880 1095 🕐 Mon–Sat 12:30–3:30, 7:30–10. Closed first week of Aug 🚌 8, 44, 46, 56, 60, 61, 64, 65, 70, 75, 81, 87, 90, 170 to Largo di Torre Argentina

PIPERNO ($$)

Much Roman cuisine is based on the city's extensive Jewish culinary traditions. The famous and resolutely traditional Piperno has been a temple to Romano-Jewish cuisine for over a century. Reserve well ahead.

➕ eIV; D6 ✉ Via Monte de' Cenci 9 ☎ 06 6880 6629/2772 🕐 Tue–Sat 12:15–2:30, 8–10:30; Sun 12:15–3. Closed Aug 🚌 8, 44, 56, 60, 65, 75, 170, 181, 710, 718, 719 to Via Arenula

GELATERIE

ALBERTO PICA

Only around 20 flavors, but of excellent quality; try the house specialties like green apple (*mele verde*) and Sicilian citrus (*agrumi di Sicilia*).

⊞ elV; C6 ✉ Via della Seggiola 12, off Via Arenula opposite Piazza Cenci ☎ 06 687 5990 🕐 Mon–Sat 8AM–1:30AM 🚌 8, 44, 56, 60, 65, 75, 170, 181, 710, 718, 719 to Via Arenula

DA MIRELLA

Sells *granita*: crushed ice drenched in juice or syrup. The flavorings in this kiosk have been refined over many years of experience, and the ice is still hand ground.

⊞ elV; D6 ✉ Lungotevere Anguillara, Ponte Cestio 🕐 Daily 8AM–late 🚌 23, 65, 280

GELATERIA DELLA PALMA

A big, brash place behind the Pantheon. Cakes and chocolates, plus over 100 flavors of ice cream—many of them wild and wonderful.

⊞ ell; D5 ✉ Via della Maddalena 20 ☎ 06 6880 6752 🕐 Daily 9AM–midnight 🚌 119 to Piazza della Rotonda

GIOLITTI

For years Giolitti was the king of Roman ice cream. Standards have slipped slightly, but the ice cream, coffee, and cakes are still excellent value.

⊞ fll; D5 ✉ Via Uffici del Vicario 40 ☎ 06 699 1243 🕐 Tue–Fri, Sun 7AM–12:30AM; Sat 7AM–2AM 🚌 119 to Piazza della Rotonda, or 52, 53, 56, 60, 62, 81, 85, 90, 160 to Via del Corso

LA FONTE DELLA SALUTE

At the so-called "Fount of Health," ice creams are made with fresh cream, sugar, eggs, and other far-from-healthful ingredients.

⊞ C7 ✉ Via Cardinale Marmaggi 2–6 🕐 Tue–Sun 8AM–10PM 🚌 8, 44, 56, 60, 75, 170, 181, 280 to Viale di Trastevere

PREMIATE GELATERIE FANTASIA

A good port of call near San Giovanni in Laterano.

⊞ G7 ✉ Via La Spezia 100–2 🕐 Mon–Sat 8AM–11PM 🚇 San Giovanni 🚌 4, 13, 16, 30, 81, 85, 87 to Piazzale Appio

SACCHETTI

Family-run bar also good for cakes and pastries.

⊞ C7 ✉ Piazza San Cosimato 61–2 ☎ 06 581 5374 🕐 Tue–Sun 5AM–11PM 🚌 8, 44, 75, 170, 181, 280, 717 to Viale di Trastevere

SAN FILIPPO

This quiet bar in Parioli is for many the best *gelateria* in the city. Zabaglione is emperor of the 60-odd flavors.

⊞ E2 ✉ Via di Villa San Filippo 8–10 ☎ 06 807 9314 🕐 Tue–Sun 7:30AM–midnight 🚌 3, 19, 30, 53, 168 to Piazza Ungheria, or 4 to Via di Villa San Filippo

TRE SCALINI

Tre Scalini is celebrated for its chocolate-studded *tartufo*, the ultimate in chocolate chip ice cream.

⊞ ell; C5 ✉ Piazza Navona 28–32 ☎ 06 6880 1996 🕐 Thu–Tue 8AM–1AM 🚌 70, 81, 87, 186, 492 to Corso del Rinascimento

Buying ice cream

Ice cream (*gelato*) in a proper *gelateria* is sold either in a cone (*un cono*) or a paper cup (*una coppa*). Specify which you want and then decide how much you wish to pay: sizes of cone and cup go up in lire bands, usually starting small and ending enormous. You can choose up to two or three flavors (more in bigger tubs) and will usually be asked if you want a swirl of cream (*panna*) to round things off.

BARS BY DAY

Bar etiquette

You almost always pay a premium to sit down (inside or outside) and to enjoy the privilege of waiter service in Roman bars. If you stand—which is cheaper—the procedure is to pay for what you want first at the cash-desk (*la cassa*). You then take your receipt (*lo scontrino*) to the bar and repeat your order (a tip slapped down on the bar will work wonders in attracting the bar person's attention). Pastry shops, cafés, and ice cream parlors often double as excellent all-around bars to be enjoyed during the day. They include Giolitti and Tre Scalini (➤ 67), Camilloni and Sant'Eustachio (➤ 69).

ALEMAGNA

A big century-old bar with a huge and varied clientele. Good self-service selection of hot and cold food.
🕇 fl; D5 ⊠ Via del Corso 181 ☎ 06 678 9135 🕓 Daily 7:30AM–11PM 🚇 Spagna 🚌 119 to Piazza Augusto Imperatore

BAR DELLA PACE

Extremely trendy, but quieter by day, when you can sit outside or enjoy the 19th-century mirror-and-mahogany interior.
🕇 ell; C5 ⊠ Via della Pace 3, off Piazza Navona ☎ 06 686 1216 🕓 Daily 9AM–2AM (closed Mon AM) 🚌 70, 81, 87, 90, 186, 492 to Corso del Rinascimento

BAR FRATTINA

A perfect retreat from shopping near Piazza di Spagna. Coffee, snacks, light meals and decadent puddings in a bustling atmosphere: some outside tables.
🕇 fl; D5 ⊠ Via Frattina 142 ☎ No phone 🕓 Mon–Sat 8PM–9PM 🚇 Spagna 🚌 119 to Piazza di Spagna

CANOVA

Canova is pricier and less atmospheric than nearby Rosati, though its sunny outside tables provide a welcome pause.
🕇 D4 ⊠ Piazza del Popolo 16 ☎ 06 361 2231 🕓 Daily 7:30AM–12:30AM 🚇 Flaminio or Spagna 🚌 119 to Piazza del Popolo

CIAMPINI

You can sit here for hours facing Bernini's Fontana dei Quattro Fiumi (➤ 54), but watch your tab.

🕇 ell; C5 ⊠ Piazza Navona 94–100 ☎ 06 686 1547 🕓 Tue–Sun 8:30AM–12:30AM 🚌 46, 62, 64 to Corso Vittorio Emanuele II or 70, 81, 87, 90, 186, 492 to Corso del Rinascimento

DONEY

Most bars famous in the *dolce vita* 1950s are now tacky and expensive. Doney, however, is as tasteful and inviting as ever.
🕇 gl; E5 ⊠ Via Vittorio Veneto 145 ☎ 06 482 1788 🕓 Tue–Sat 8AM–1AM 🚇 Barberini 🚌 52, 53, 56, 58, 95 to Via Vittorio Veneto

LATTERIA DEL GALLO

Old-fashioned, with original marble tables and 1940s decor. Try the big, sticky cakes and steaming hot chocolate.
🕇 dll; C6 ⊠ Vicolo del Gallo 4 ☎ 06 686 5091 🕓 Thu–Tue 8:30–2, 5–midnight 🚌 46, 62, 64 to Corso Vittorio Emanuele II

ROSATI

Wonderful coffee, cocktails, cakes and pastries (from vintage ovens), and a glittering 1922 art nouveau interior.
🕇 D4 ⊠ Piazza del Popolo 5 ☎ 06 322 5859 🕓 Daily 7:30AM–midnight 🚇 Flaminio or Spagna 🚌 119 to Piazza del Popolo

TRASTÈ

This chic tea and coffee shop in Trastevere also serves light meals. People come to chat, read the papers, and pass the hours.
🕇 elV; C6 ⊠ Via della Lungaretta 76 ☎ 06 589 4430 🕓 Tue–Sun 5PM–12:30AM 🚌 8, 44, 56, 60, 75, 170, 181, 280, 717 to Piazza Sidney Sonnino

COFFEE & PASTRIES

ANTICO CAFFÈ BRASILE
Superb variety of beans and ground coffee sold from huge sacks or at the bar. Try the "Pope's blend": John Paul II bought his coffee here before his pontificate.
✠ hIII; E6 ✉ Via dei Serpenti 23 ☎ 06 488 2319 🕐 Mon–Sat 6:30AM–8:30PM 🚌 57, 64, 65, 70, 75, 81, 170 to Via Nazionale

BABINGTON'S TEA ROOMS
Only tourists and the well-heeled visit Babington's, established by a pair of English spinsters in 1896. Prices are sky-high, but the tea (although not the cakes) is the best in Rome.
✠ fI; D5 ✉ Piazza di Spagna 23 ☎ 06 678 6027 🕐 Wed–Mon 9AM–8PM Ⓜ Spagna 🚌 119 to Piazza di Spagna

CAFÉ NOTEGEN
This friendly old family-run café has a loyal local clientele. Excellent light lunches and all-day snacks to take out or eat in.
✠ D4 ✉ Via del Babuino 159 ☎ 06 320 0855 🕐 Mon–Sat 7AM–midnight; Sun 10:30AM–midnight Ⓜ Spagna 🚌 119 to Piazza del Popolo

CAFFÈ FARNESE
Quieter and more elegant than the bars on the nearby Campo de' Fiori. Serves cakes, ice creams, and light snacks as well as drinks. Also has tables on the cobbled street outside.
✠ eIII; C6 ✉ Via dei Baullari 106–7, at Piazza Farnese ☎ 06 6880 2125 🕐 Daily 7AM–2AM 🚌 8, 44, 56, 60, 75, 170

CAFFÈ GRECO
Rome's most famous café, founded in 1767. Plush, but no longer the best.
✠ fI; D5 ✉ Via dei Condotti 86 ☎ 06 678 5474 🕐 Mon–Sat 8AM–9PM Ⓜ Spagna 🚌 119 to Piazza di Spagna, or 52, 53, 58, 61, 71, 85, 160 to Piazza San Silvestro

CAMILLONI
A long-time rival to Sant'Eustachio, with which it shares a piazza.
✠ eIII; D5 ✉ Piazza Sant' Eustachio 54 ☎ 06 271 6068 🕐 Tue–Sun 8AM–9PM 🚌 119 to Piazza della Rotonda, or 70, 81, 87, 186, 492 to Corso del Rinascimento

DAGNINO
Not even the customers have changed in this superb 1950s *pasticceria*. Fine Sicilian specialties, lemon ices, and ice cream.
✠ hI; E5 ✉ Galleria Esedra, Via Vittorio Emanuele Orlando 75 ☎ 06 481 8660 🕐 Daily 7AM–10PM Ⓜ Spagna 🚌 57, 64, 65, 75, 170, 492, 910 to Piazza della Repubblica

LA TAZZA D'ORO
The "Cup of Gold" sells only coffee, and probably the city's best espresso.
✠ eIII; D5 ✉ Via degli Orfani 84 ☎ 06 678 9792 🕐 Mon–Sat 7AM–8PM 🚌 119 to Piazza della Rotonda, or 70, 81, 87, 90, 186, 492 to Corso del Rinascimento

SANT'EUSTACHIO
Rivals La Tazza d'Oro, with a pleasant interior and tables outside.
✠ eIII; D5 ✉ Piazza Sant' Eustachio 82 ☎ 06 686 1309 🕐 Tue–Sun 8:30AM–1AM 🚌 119 to Piazza della Rotonda, or 70, 81, 87, 90, 186, 492 to Corso del Rinascimento

Breakfast and coffee
Breakfast in Rome consists of a sweet, sometimes cream-filled croissant (*un cornetto* or *brioche*) washed down with a cappuccino or the longer and milkier *caffè latte*. At other times espresso, a short kick-start of caffeine, is the coffee of choice (Italians never drink cappuccino after lunch or dinner). Decaffeinated coffee is *caffè Hag*, iced coffee *caffè freddo*, and American-style coffee (long and watery) *caffè Americano*. Other varieties include *caffè corretto* (with a dash of grappa or brandy) and *caffè macchiato* (espresso "stained" with a dash of milk).

69

FOOTWEAR

Shopping areas

Although Rome's individual neighborhoods have their own butchers, bakers, and corner shops (*alimentari*), most of the city's quality and specialty shops are concentrated in specific areas. Via Condotti and its surrounding grid of streets (Via Frattina, Via Borgognona, and Via Bocca di Leone) contain most of the big names in men's and women's fashion, accessories, jewelry, and luxury goods. In nearby Via del Babuino and Via Margutta, the emphasis is on top antiques, paintings, sculpture, and modern glassware and lighting. Via della Croce, which runs south from Piazza di Spagna, is known for its food shops, while Via del Corso, which bisects the northern half of central Rome, is home to bargain mid-range clothes, shoes, and accessories stores. Inexpensive stores can be found along Via del Tritone and Via Nazionale. Nice areas to browse for antiques, even if you are not buying, include Via Giulia, Via dei Coronari, Via dell'Orso, Via dei Soldati, and Via del Governo Vecchio.

BATA
A well-known and respected chain devoted predominantly to casual footwear. It also sells children's shoes.
🛒 gl; D5 ✉ Via dei Due Macelli 45 ☎ 06 679 1570 🕐 Tue–Sat 9:30–7:30; Mon 3:30–7:30
🛒 hll; E5 ✉ Via Nazionale 89 ☎ 06 482 4529 🕐 Tue–Sat 9:30–7:30; Mon 3:30–7:30

BRUNO MAGLI
A middle- to upscale quality chain with a choice of formal and some casual styles.
🛒 fl; D5 ✉ Via del Gambero 1 ☎ 06 779 3802 🕐 Tue–Sat 9:30–7:30; Mon 1–7:30
🛒 gl; E5 ✉ Via Vittorio Veneto 70a ☎ 06 488 4355 🕐 Tue–Sat 9:30–7:30; Mon 1–7:30
🛒 off map to southwest ✉ Aeroporto di Fiumicino ☎ 06 6501 1730 🕐 Tue–Sat 9:30–7:30; Mon 1–7:30

CAMPANILE
This shop, in chic Via dei Condotti, is dedicated to the most elegant (and expensive) styles. Men's and women's shoes, plus a range of leather bags.
🛒 fl; D5 ✉ Via Condotti 58 ☎ 06 678 3041 🕐 Tue–Sat 9:30–7:30; Mon 3:30–7:30

FAUSTO SANTINI
An iconoclast who designs witty, innovative, and occasionally bizarre shoes for the young and daring.
🛒 fl; D5 ✉ Via Frattina 120–1 ☎ 06 678 4114 🕐 Tue–Sat 10–7:30; Mon 3:30–7:30

FERRAGAMO
An established family firm; probably Italy's best-known shoe store, with branches on exclusive shopping streets the world over.
🛒 fl; D5 ✉ Via dei Condotti 73–4 ☎ 06 679 1565 🛒 fl, D5 ✉ Via Condotti 64 ☎ 06 678 1130 🕐 Tue–Sat 10–7; Mon 3–7:30

FRATELLI ROSSETTI
This family company, founded 30 years ago by the brothers Renzo and Renato, rivals Ferragamo as Italy's best shoe store, and is slightly cheaper. Classic and current styles for men and women.
🛒 fl; D5 ✉ Via Borgognona 5a ☎ 06 678 2676 🕐 Tue–Sat 9:30–7:30; Mon 3:30–7:30

POLLINI
Up-to-the minute boots and bags in lively styles for men and women.
🛒 fl; D5 ✉ Via Frattina 22–4 ☎ 06 678 9028 🕐 Tue–Sat 10–1, 3–7:30; Mon 3–7:30

RAMIREZ
Via del Corso is dotted with excellent cheap and mid-range shoe stores; Ramirez is one of the best. A huge range of up-to-the-minute styles for men and women, plus bags and accessories.
🛒 fll; D5 ✉ Via del Corso 176 ☎ 06 679 5928 🕐 Tue–Sun 9–8, Mon 4–8

TOD'S
Distinctive and much-coveted driving shoes made Tod's a big fashion label. A showcase store for an ever-expanding range of quality shoes, both smart and informal.
🛒 fl; D5 ✉ Via Borgognona 45 ☎ 06 678 6828 🕐 Tue–Sat 10–7:30, Mon 3:30–7:30

ACCESSORIES & LEATHER GOODS

BORSALINO
This shop should be your first port of call if you are looking to buy a hat.
🞧 D4 ✉ Piazza del Popolo 20
☎ 06 679 4192
🕑 Mon–Sat 9–8

CALZA E CALZE
A cornucopia of socks, stockings, and tights in every color and style imaginable.
🞧 fI; D5 ✉ Via della Croce 78
🕑 Tue–Sat 9:30–1, 3:30–7:30;
Mon 3:30–7:30

FENDI
A famous family-run high-fashion name whose burgeoning Via Borgognana shop deals in both clothes and fine leather goods.
🞧 fI; D5 ✉ Via Borgognona
36a–39 ☎ 06 679 7641
🕑 Mon–Sat 10–7:30

FOGAL
A small store crammed with a dazzling selection of tights, stockings, socks and lingerie: choose between conservative or more innovative styles and colors.
🞧 fI; D5 ✉ Via dei Condotti
55 ☎ 06 678 4566
🕑 Tue–Sat 10–7:30, Mon
1:30–3:30

GUCCI
Recovering from the turmoil of the 1980s, when tax problems and feuds threatened to destroy the family business, this famous name is once more in the ascendant. Expensive and high-quality bags, shoes, and leather goods are a feature of this elegant shop.

🞧 fI; D5 ✉ Via Condotti 8
☎ 06 678 9340 🕑 Tue–Sat
10–2, 3–7; Mon 3–7

LA PERLA
Italian lingerie is among the best in the world, and its reputation is upheld by La Perla. Wonderful fabrics, and a variety of colors and styles, plus sizes to suit all.
🞧 fI; D5 ✉ Via dei Condotti 79
☎ 06 6994 1934 🕑 Tue–Sat
9:30–7:30, Mon 3:30–7:30

MEROLA
Specializes in a wide range of highly priced gloves, scarves, and panty hose.
🞧 fI; D5 ✉ Via del Corso 143
☎ 06 679 1961 🕑 Tue–Sat
9:30–7:30; Mon 3:30–7:30

SERGIO DI CORI
Romans who need gloves look no further than this tiny shop, which sells almost nothing else.
🞧 fI; D5 ✉ Piazza di Spagna
53 ☎ 06 678 4439 🕑 Tue–Sat
9:30–7:30; Mon 1–7:30

SERMONETA
Glove specialist: styles are innovative and colors bright—fuchsias, purples and vivid reds—although the store is not as famous as nearby rival, Sergio di Cori.
🞧 fI; D5 ✉ Piazza di Spagna
61 ☎ 06 679 1960 🕑 Tue–Sat
9:30–7:30; Mon 1–7:30

SIRNI
Exquisite artisan-made bags and briefcases crafted on the premises.
🞧 D5 ✉ Via della Stelletta 33
☎ 06 6880 5248 🕑 Tue–Sat
9:30–1:30, 3:30–7:30; Mon
3:30–7:30

Jewelry

Jewelry, and lots of it, is a key part of any Roman woman's wardrobe. Gold, in particular, is popular, and is still worked in small artisans' studios in the Jewish Ghetto, around Via Giulia and Campo de' Fiori and on Via dei Coronari, Via dell'Orso, and Via del Pellegrino. For the purchase of a lifetime, visit the most famous of Italian jewelers, Bulgari, whose shop at Via Condotti 10 is one of the most splendid in the city. For striking costume jewelry try Delettré (✉ Via Fontanella Borghese) or Bozart (✉ Via Bocca di Leone 4). For a more sober look visit Massoni (✉ Largo Carlo Goldoni 48), founded in 1790, or Petocchi (✉ Piazza di Spagna), jewelers to Italy's former royal family from 1861 to 1946.

WOMEN'S FASHION

Sales and bargaining

Sales (*saldi*) in Rome are not always the bargains they can be in other major cities. That said, many shoe stores and top designers cut their prices drastically during summer and winter sales (mid-July to mid-September and January to mid-March). Other lures to get you into a shop, notably the offer of *sconti* (discounts) and *vendite promozionali* (promotional offers), rarely save you any money. While bargaining has all but died out, it can still occasionally be worth asking for a discount (*uno sconto*), particularly if you are paying cash (as opposed to using a credit card) for an expensvie item, or if you are buying several items from one shop.

FENDI

From recent beginnings, the Fendi sisters have built a powerful fashion, perfume, and accessories empire. Clothes are classic, sleek, and stylish.

fl; D5 ⊠ Via Borgognona 36a–39 ☎ 06 679 7641 ⏰ Mon–Sat 10–7:30

GIANFRANCO FERRÈ

One of Italy's top designers. His Rome shop is known for its outlandish steel and black mosaic decor.

fl; D5 ⊠ Via Borgognona 6 ☎ 06 679 0050 ⏰ Tue–Sat 9:30–7:30; Mon 3:30–7:30

GIANNI VERSACE

Flashier and trashier than Ferrè or Armani, Versace's bright, bold styles take panache. The cheaper diffusion range, Versus, has an outlet at Via Borgognona 33–4.

fl; D5 ⊠ Via Bocca di Leone 25 ☎ 06 678 0521 ⏰ Tue–Sat 10–7:30; Mon 3:30–7:30

GIORGIO ARMANI

King of cut and classic, understated elegance. The slightly cheaper line is at Emporio Armani (➤ 73).

fl; D5 ⊠ Via dei Condotti 77 ☎ 06 699 1460 ⏰ Mon 3:30–7:30; Tue–Sat 10–7

MARELLA

The showcase shop for the Marella label offers well-made and extremely wearable designs at reasonable prices. The classic styling appeals to young and old alike.

fl; D5 ⊠ Via Frattina 129–31 ☎ 06 6992 3800 ⏰ Tue–Sat 10–7:30; Mon 3:30–7:30

LAURA BIAGIOTTI

Easy to wear, easy on the eye and less aggressively "high fashion" than the other outlets in Via Borgognona.

fl; D5 ⊠ Via Borgognona 43–44 ☎ 06 679 1205 ⏰ Tue–Sat 10–7:30; Mon 3:30–7:30

MAX MARA

A popular mid-range label known for reliable suits, separates, knitwear, and bags and other accessories at fair prices. See also sister shop, Max & Co., at Via dei Condotti 46–46a.

fl; D5 ⊠ Via dei Condotti 46 ☎ 06 678 7946 ⏰ Tue–Sat 10–7:30; Mon 3:30–7:30

fl; D5 ⊠ Via Frattina 28 ☎ 06 679 3638 ⏰ Tue–Sat 10–7:30; Mon 3:30–7:30

TRUSSARDI

Flagship store for another top name in Italian fashion.

fl; D5 ⊠ Via Condotti 49 ☎ 06 679 2151 ⏰ Tue–Sat 10–7:30; Mon 3:30–7:30

VALENTINO

The maestro of Roman fashion has been dressing celebrities and the rich since 1959. For more affordable ready-to-wear creations visit Via dei Condotti and Via Bocca di Leone, and, for the still cheaper Oliver line, Via del Babuino 61 (➤ 77).

fl; D5 ⊠ Piazza Mignanelli 22 ☎ 06 67 391 ⏰ Tue–Sat 10–2, 3:30–7:30; Mon 10–2

fl; D5 ⊠ Via Bocca di Leone 15 ☎ 06 679 5862 ⏰ Tue–Sat 10–2, 3:30–7:30; Mon 10–2

fl; D5 ⊠ Via dei Condotti 12 ☎ 06 6783 3656 ⏰ Tue–Sat 10–2, 3:30–7:30; Mon 10–2

Men's Tailors & Clothes

BATTISTONI

This traditional tailor's shop has sold made-to-measure and ready-to-wear suits and shirts for over half a century. Also stocks well-made informal wear.

✚ fl; D5 ✉ Via Condotti 57 and 61a ☎ 06 678 6241 ◷ Tue–Sat 9:30–1:30, 3:30–7:30; Mon 3:30–7:30

DAVIDE CENCI

The country gentleman look—tweeds, brogues, and muted classics—is hugely popular among Italian men. This enormous store, established in 1926, caters to the trend with Burberry, Aquascutum, and its own lines.

◷ ell; D5 ✉ Via Campo Marzio 1–7 ☎ 06 699 0681 ◷ Tue–Sat 9–1, 3:30–7:30; Mon 3:30–7:30

DIESEL

A large, modern mid-range store aimed at the young or young at heart which sells its fashionable own-label jeans, shirts, and other informal wear.

✚ fl; D5 ✉ Via del Corso 186 ☎ 06 678 3933 ◷ Tue–Sat 10:30–7:30; Sun 3–7:30; Mon 2–7:30

EMPORIO ARMANI

Relatively speaking, the cheaper way to buy Armani.

✚ D4 ✉ Via del Babuino 139–40 ☎ 06 678 8454 ◷ Mon–Sat 10–7

ENZO CECI

Ready-to-wear high fashion.

✚ fl; D5 ✉ Via della Vite 52 ☎ 06 679 8882 ◷ Tue–Sat 9:30–1:30, 3:30–7:30; Mon 3:30–7:30

ERMENEGILDO ZEGNA

Informal suits and jackets in exquisite, expensive fabrics. Also stocks shirts, sweaters and accessories.

✚ fl; D5 ✉ Via Borgognona 7e ☎ 06 678 9143 ◷ Tue–Sat 10–7:30, Mon 3:30–7:30

SCHOSTAL

Conservative clothes and accessories, beautifully made in the finest fabrics. Surprisingly favorable prices, with courteous, old-fashioned service.

✚ fl; D5 ✉ Via del Corso 158 ☎ 06 679 1240 ◷ Tue–Sat 9:30–7:30, Mon 3:30–7:30

TESTA

Exquisite suits cut to appeal to a younger set, plus an excellent range of (mostly blue) shirts.

✚ fl; D5 ✉ Via Borgognona 13 ☎ 06 679 6174 ✚ fl; D5 ✉ Via Frattina 104 ☎ 06 679 1296 ◷ Tue–Sat 9:30–1:30, 3:30–7:30; Mon 3:30–7:30

VALENTINO UOMO

Sober and conservative clothes in the finest materials from Rome's leading tailor.

✚ fl; D5 ✉ Via Condotti 12 ☎ 06 6783 3656 ◷ Tue–Sat 10–2, 3:30–7:30; Mon 3:30–7:30

Oliver ✚ D4 ✉ Via del Babuino 61 ☎ 06 3600 1906 ◷ Tue–Sat 10–2, 3:30–7:30; Mon 3:30–7:30

VERSACE UOMO

Bold, sexy clothes for lounge lizards and aspirant pop stars.

✚ fl; D5 ✉ Via Borgognona 33–4 ☎ 06 678 3977 ◷ Tue–Sat 10–7:30; Mon 3:30–7:30

Top people's tailor

While the young turn to the mainstream Milanese designers like Armani, Rome's older and more traditional élite still choose Battistoni for their sartorial needs. Giorgio Battistoni started out almost half a century ago as a shirtmaker, but quickly graduated to the role of top-class tailor, dressing the city's older aristocracy and the more conservative hedonists of the late 1950s *dolce vita*. Clothes with the Battistoni label are still as prestigious as they were in the past, and just as costly—a custom-made shirt starts at around L300,000.

BOOKS & STATIONERY

Foreign newspapers

Foreign newspapers can be bought at many newsstands (*edicole*) around the city. European editions of the *International Herald Tribune* and the *Financial Times* (and occasionally *USA Today*) hit the newsstands first thing in the morning with the Italian papers. Other foreign editions arrive at around 2:30PM on the day of issue, except for Sunday editions, which are not usually available until Monday morning. The best-stocked newsstands, which also include a wide range of foreign magazines and periodicals, are found in Piazza Colonna on Via del Corso, at Termini train station, and at the southern end of the Via Vittorio Veneto.

ECONOMY BOOK AND VIDEO CENTER
Italy's largest English-language bookstore is an established fixture of expat life. New and secondhand titles are available. Pricey.
🕂 hII; E5 ✉ Via Torino 136
☎ 06 474 6877 🕔 Mon–Fri 9:30–7:30; Sat 9:30–1:30

FELTRINELLI
An Italy-wide bookstore chain, with well-designed shops and shelves displaying a broad range of Italian titles, and usually a reasonable choice of French-, German-, and English-language books.
🕂 eIII; C6 ✉ Largo di Torre Argentina 5a ☎ 06 6880 3248
🕔 Mon–Sat 9–8; Sun 10–1:30, 4–7:30
🕂 D4 ✉ Via del Babuino 39–40
☎ 06 679 7058 🕔 Mon–Sat 9–8; Sun 10–1:30, 4–7:30
🕂 hI; E5 ✉ Via Vittorio Emanuele II Orlando 84–6 ☎ 06 484 430 🕔 Mon–Sat 9–8; Sun 10–1:30, 4–7:30

IL SIGILLO
Close to the Pantheon, this little shop specializes in fine pens, hand-printed stationery and a wide variety of objects covered in marbled paper.
🕂 eII; D5 ✉ Via della Guglia 69 ☎ 06 678 9667 🕔 Tue–Sat 11–7:30; Mon 3:30–7:30

MONDADORI
This showcase shop for one of Italy's largest publishing houses sells books, maps, and music, plus videos, posters, and greeting cards.
🕂 C4 ✉ Piazza Cola di Rienzo 81–3 ☎ 06 321 60895
🕔 Mon–Sat 9:30–7:30

PINEIDER
Rome's most expensive and exclusive stationers. Virtually any design can be printed onto personalized visiting or business cards.
🕂 gI; D5 ✉ Via dei Due Macelli 68 ☎ 06 678 9013
🕔 Tue–Sat 10–2, 3–7; Mon 3–7
🕂 fI; D5 ✉ Via della Fontanella Borghese 22 ☎ 06 687 8369
🕔 Tue–Sat 10–2, 3–7; Mon 3–7

POGGI
Vivid pigments, lovely papers, and exquisitely soft brushes have been on sale at Poggi's since 1825.
🕂 fIII; D6 ✉ Via del Gesù 74–5
☎ 06 678 4477 🕔 Mon–Fri 9–1, 4–7:30; Sat 9–1
🕂 fIII; D5 ✉ Via Piè di Marmo 40–1 ☎ 06 6830 8014
🕔 Mon–Fri 9–1, 4–7:30; Sat 9–1

RIZZOLI
Italy's largest bookstore appears dated alongside newer rivals, but you should be able to find any Italian book in print (as well as a selection in English).
🕂 fI; D5 ✉ Galleria Colonna, Largo Chigi 15 ☎ 06 679 6641
🕔 Mon–Sat 9–7; Sun 10:30–1:25, 4–7:55

VERTECCHI
The best source of stationery, napkins, wrapping paper, boxes, obelisks, and books covered in beautiful Florentine marbled paper.
🕂 fI; D5 ✉ Via della Croce 70
☎ 06 678 3110 🕔 Tue–Sat 9–7:30; Mon 3:30–7:30
🕂 C4 ✉ Via dei Gracchi 179
☎ 06 321 3559 🕔 Tue–Sat 9–7:30; Mon 3:30–7:30

CHINA, GLASS & FABRIC

BISES

A breathtaking range of fabrics is housed in an elegant 17th-century *palazzo* in Via del Gesù. Bises specializes in high-fashion fabrics such as silk, wool, and velvet, but also stocks a range of home furnishing materials.

🔲 flll; D6 🖂 Via del Gesù 63 ☎ 06 678 9156 🕐 Tue–Sat 9:30–1, 3:30–7:30; Mon 3:30–7:30

CESARI

Cesari sells a wide range of outstanding linen and lingerie, but is better known for its fabrics, especially furnishing materials. The shop's setting is almost as beautiful as the products on sale.

🔲 D4 🖂 Via del Babuino 16 ☎ 06 361 1441 🕐 Tue–Sat 9:30–1, 3:30–7:30; Mon 3:30–7:30

BASSETTI

Central store with a dazzling collection of high-quality Italian silks and other luxurious fabrics, plus everyday materials.

🔲 dlll; C6 🖂 Corso Vittorio Emanuele II 73 ☎ 06 689 2326 🕐 Tue–Sat 9–7:30, Mon 3:30–7:30 🚌 46, 62, 64

CULTI

Store near Piazza Navona packed with linens, well-designed kitchen utensils, plates, glasses, vases, towels, sheets, and a host of other articles for the home.

🔲 ell; C5 🖂 Via della Vetrina 16a ☎ 06 683 2180 🕐 Tue–Sat 10–1:30, 4–7:30; Mon 4–7:30 🚇 Spagna 🚌 70, 81, 87, 186 to Corso della Rinascimento

FRETTE

This chain is a by-word across Italy for the finest towels, sheets, and household linens. Prices are high, but the quality is excellent.

🔲 fl; D5 🖂 Via del Corso 381 ☎ 06 678 6862 🕐 Tue–Sat 9:30–7:30, Mon 3:30–7:30 🚇 Spagna 🚌 52, 53, 56, 58 and other services to Via del Tritone or Piazza San Silvestro

🔲 hll; E5 🖂 Via Nazionale 84 ☎ 06 488 2641 🕐 Tue–Sat 9:30–7:30, Mon 3:30–7:30 🚇 Repubblica 🚌 57, 64, 65, 70, 75, 170

GINORI

One of the top Italian names in modern and traditional glass and china.

🔲 gl; D5 🖂 Piazza Trinità dei Monti 18b ☎ 06 679 3836 🕐 Tue–Sat 10–7:30

🔲 gl; D5 🖂 Via del Tritone 177 ☎ 06 679 3836 🕐 Tue–Sat 10–7:30

SPAZIO SETTE

On three floors at the splendid Palazzo Lazzaroni are superbly designed objects ranging from candles to clocks and corkscrews.

🔲 elll; C6 🖂 Via dei Barbieri 7 ☎ 06 6880 4261 🕐 Tue–Sat 9:30–1, 3:30–7:30; Mon 3:30–7:30

STILVETRO

Italian glassware and china, much of it from Tuscany, make this established shop a good source for authentic and inexpensive gifts.

🔲 fl; D5 🖂 Via Frattina 56 ☎ 06 679 0258 🕐 Tue–Sat 9:30–2, 2:30–7:30; Mon 3:30–7:30

Gifts with a twist

For a souvenir with a difference, visit the extraordinary shops on Via dei Cestari, just south of the Pantheon, which specialize in all sorts of religious clothes, candles, and vestments. Crucifixes, rosaries, statues of saints and other religious souvenirs can be found in shops on Via di Porta Angelica near the Vatican. Alternatively, visit the Farmacia Santa Maria della Scala (🖂 Piazza Santa Maria della Scala), an 18th-century monastic pharmacy that sells herbal remedies.

For interesting toys, try: **Città del Sole** 🖂 Via della Scrofa 65 ☎ 06 6880 3805 🖂 Piazza Chiesa Nuova 22 ☎ 06 687 2922

For the best in old prints and engravings investigate: **Pacitti** 🖂 Via dei Banchi Vecchi 59 ☎ 06 6880 6391 **L'Impronta** 🖂 Via del Teatro Valle 53 ☎ 06 686 7821

FOOD & WINE

Local shopping

Roman supermarkets are few and far between (see panel opposite), and most food is still bought in tiny neighborhood shops known as *alimentari*. Every street of every "village" or district in the city has one or more of these general stores, a source of everything from olive oil and pasta to candles and corn and bunion treatments. They are also good places to buy picnic provisions—many sell bread and wine—and most have a delicatessen counter that will make you a sandwich (*panino*) from the meats and cheeses on display. For something a little more special, or for food gifts to take home, visit Via della Croce, a street renowned for its wonderful delicatessens. In addition to Salumeria Focacci, note the excellent Fratelli Fabbi (⊠ Via della Croce 27); and Fior Fiore (⊠ Via della Croce 17–18), known for its pizzas, pastas, and pastries.

AI MONASTERI
This unusual, large and rather dark old shop sells the products of seven Italian monasteries, from honeys, wines, natural preserves, and liqueurs to herbal cures and elixirs.
✚ ell; C5 ⊠ Piazza Cinque Lune 76 ☎ 06 6880 2783 ⏰ Mon–Wed, Fri, Sat 9–1, 4:40–7:30; Thu 9–1. Closed first week of Sep

CASTRONI
Castroni boasts Rome's largest selection of imported delicacies, a mouthwatering array of Italian specialties and an outstanding range of coffees.
✚ C4 ⊠ Via Cola di Rienzo 196 ☎ 06 687 4383 ⏰ Mon–Sat 8–8

CATENA
Founded in 1928, this luxury food store sells Italian hams, cheeses, coffees, regional delicacies, vintage wines and liqueurs.
✚ F7 ⊠ Via Appia Nuova 9 ☎ 06 7049 1664 ⏰ Tue–Sat 9:30–1, 3:30–7:30; Mon 3:30–7:30

ENOTECA BUCCONE
Rome's most select and best-stocked wine shop occupies a 17th-century coach house.
✚ D4 ⊠ Via di Ripetta 19–20 ☎ 06 361 2154 ⏰ Daily 9–8:30. Closed Aug

ENOTECA AL GOCCETTO
Wines from all over Italy are sold in this old bishop's *palazzo*, complete with original floors and wooden ceiling.
✚ dll; C5 ⊠ Via dei Banchi Vecchi 14 ☎ 06 686 4268 ⏰ Mon–Sat 10:30–1:30, 5–9

PIETRO FRANCHI
A rival to nearby Castroni as Rome's best delicatessen. Offers a selection of regional food and wines, and dishes to take out—anything from cold antipasti to succulent roast meats.
✚ C4 ⊠ Via Cola di Rienzo 204 ☎ 06 686 4576 ⏰ Mon–Sat 8AM–9PM

ROFFI ISABELLI
A beautiful old-fashioned shop where you can buy wine by the bottle or sip it by the glass amid trickling fountains and marble-topped tables.
✚ fl; D5 ⊠ Via della Croce 76b ☎ 06 679 0896 ⏰ Daily 11AM–midnight

SALUMERIA FOCACCI
For variety and quality, this is one of the best in a street renowned for its food shops (*salumeria* means delicatessen; *salumi* are cold cuts). See panel, left, for other good establishments nearby.
✚ fl; D5 ⊠ Via della Croce 43 ☎ 06 679 1228 ⏰ Mon–Wed, Fri, Sat 8:30–1:30, 4:30–7:30; Thu 8:30–1:30

VINCENZO TASCIONI
This most famous of Roman neighborhood shops sells fresh pasta in over 30 different varieties, all made on the premises.
✚ C4 ⊠ Via Cola di Rienzo 211 ☎ 06 324 3152 ⏰ Mon–Wed, Fri, Sat 8–2, 4–8; Thu 4–8

STREET MARKETS

CAMPO DE' FIORI

This picturesque market is in a pretty, central square. Fruit and vegetables dominate, but you can also buy fish, flowers, and beans.

🞤 ell; C6 ⊠ Piazza Campo de' Fiori ⊙ Mon–Sat 7AM–1:30PM

MERCATO ANDREA DORIA

A large, local market which serves the neighborhood residents northwest of the Vatican. Stands sell meat, fish, fruit, and vegetables, but there are a few with shoes and quality clothes.

🞤 B4 ⊠ Via Andrea Doria-Via Tunisi ⊙ Mon–Sat 7AM–1PM

MERCATO DEI FIORI

Not to be confused with Campo de' Fiori, this wholesale flower market in a covered hall is open to the public only on Tuesdays. Prices are reasonable for cut flowers, potted plants, and Mediterranean blooms.

🞤 B4 ⊠ Via Trionfale 47–9 ⊙ Tue 10:30AM–1PM

MERCATO DI PIAZZA VITTORIO

Stallholders in central Rome's biggest and most colorful general market are fighting plans to restore the square to its 19th-century grandeur and move the stalls to nearby Via Giolitti.

🞤 F6 ⊠ Piazza Vittorio Emanuele II ⊙ Mon–Sat 7AM–2PM

MERCATO DELLE STAMPE

Tucked away, about a dozen stalls sell old books, magazines, and prints (*stampe* in Italian). Be prepared to haggle.

🞤 el; D5 ⊠ Largo della Fontanella di Borghese ⊙ Mon–Sat 9–5:30

MERCATO DI VIA SANNIO

This market in the shadow of San Giovanni in Laterano sells bags, belts, shoes, toys, and cheap clothes. Stands nearby peddle more interesting bric-a-brac and secondhand clothes.

🞤 F7 ⊠ Via Sannio ⊙ Mon–Fri 10–1:30; Sat 10–6

PIAZZA COPPELLE

This tiny, attractive local food market is an oasis among the cars and tourists. Close to the Pantheon.

🞤 ell; D5 ⊠ Piazza Coppelle ⊙ Mon–Sat 7AM–1PM

PIAZZA SAN COSIMATO

Few visitors manage to find this mid-sized general neighborhood food market in Trastevere.

🞤 C7 ⊠ Piazza San Cosimato ⊙ Mon–Sat 7AM–1PM

PORTA PORTESE

Everything and anything is for sale in this famous flea market, though the few genuine antiques are highly priced. By mid-morning, crowds are huge, so come early and guard your belongings.

🞤 C7 ⊠ Via Porta Portese-Via Ippolito Nuevo ⊙ Sun 6:30AM–2PM

Supermarkets

At the other extreme to Rome's sprawling markets are its handful of supermarkets and department stores, both types of shop that are still rather alien to most Italians. The best department store is La Rinascente, which has a central branch at Via del Corso 189, and another in Piazza Fiume. Coin is also good, though a little less stylish, and is close to San Giovanni in Laterano at Piazzale Appio 15. Cheaper again are the large Upim and Standa chains, which offer reasonably priced clothes and general household goods. Upim has branches at Via del Tritone 172, Via Nazionale 211 and Piazza Santa Maria Maggiore; Standa's Rome branches are at Viale Trastevere 62–4, Via Appia Nuova 181–3, and Via Cola di Rienzo 173.

BARS BY NIGHT

What to drink

The cheapest way to drink beer in Italy is from the keg (*alla spina*). Measures are *piccola*, *media*, and *grande* (usually 33cl, 50cl, and a liter respectively). Foreign canned or bottled beers (*in lattina* or *in bottiglia*) are expensive. Italian brands like Peroni are a little cheaper: a Peroncino (25cl bottle) is a good thirst-quencher. Aperitifs (*aperitivi*) include popular non-alcoholic drinks like Aperol, Crodino, and San Pellegrino bitter. A glass of red or white wine is *un bicchiere di vino rosso/bianco*.

BAR DELLA PACE
(► 68)

BEVITORIA
Friendlier and more intimate than most large or touristy bars on Piazza Navona. Primarily a wine bar (the cellar is part of Domitian's former stadium). Gets busy, so arrive early.
✚ elI; C5 ⊠ Piazza Navona 72 ☎ 06 6880 1022 🕔 Mon–Sat 2PM–1AM 🚌 46, 62, 64 to Corso Vittorio Emanuele II, or 70, 81, 87, 90 to Corso del Rinascimento

CAVOUR 313
At the Forum end of Via Cavour, this easily missed wine bar has a relaxed, student feel. Good snacks from the bar, and wine by the glass or bottle, at tables to the rear. A good alternative to tourist bars nearby.
✚ glII; E6 ⊠ Via Cavour 313 ☎ 06 678 5496 🕔 Mon–Sat 10–3:30, 7:30–11:30 🚌 11, 27, 81 to Via Cavour, or 85, 87, 186 to Via dei Fori Imperiali

CUL DE SAC
An established informal wine bar near Piazza Navona with pine tables and a big marble bar. More than 1,400 wines, plus first-rate snacks, light meals, and cheese and salami from every region in Italy.
✚ elI–elII; C5 ⊠ Piazza Pasquino 73 ☎ 06 6880 1094 🕔 Tue–Sat 12:30PM–3, 6:30–12:30AM 🚌 46, 62, 64 to Corso Vittorio Emanuele II

DOG AND DUCK
English- and Irish-style pubs are all the rage in Rome. This is one of the better Trastevere versions.
✚ elV; C7 ⊠ Via della Luce 70 ☎ 06 589 5173 🕔 Sun–Thu 7:30PM–2AM, Fri–Sat 7:30PM–3AM 🚌 8, 44, 56, 60, 75, 170

DRUID'S DEN
Friendly and realistic Irish pub that appeals to Romans and expats alike. Also try The Fiddler's Elbow, a popular sister pub around the corner at Via dell'Olmata 43.
✚ E6 ⊠ Via San Martino ai Monti 28 ☎ 06 4890 4781 🕔 Mon–Fri 5PM–12:30AM, Sat, Sun 4PM–1AM 🚇 Cavour 🚌 11 to Via Giovanni Lanza, or 27, 81 to Via Cavour, or 4, 9, 14, 16 to Piazza Santa Maria Maggiore

IL PICCOLO
This intimate and pretty little wine bar close to Piazza Navona is ideal for a romantic interlude.
✚ dII; C5 ⊠ Via del Governo Vecchio 74–5 ☎ 06 6880 1746 🕔 Mon–Fri 11AM–2AM; Sat, Sun 7PM–2AM 🚌 46, 62, 64 to Corso Vittorio Emanuele II

LA VINERIA REGGIO
The quainter side of night-time drinking. Fusty and old-fashioned inside, with characters to match; tables on the city's most evocative square.
✚ elII; C6 ⊠ Campo de' Fiori 15 ☎ 06 6880 3268 🕔 Mon–Sat 10AM–4PM, 6PM–2AM 🚌 46, 62, 64 to Corso Vittorio Emanuele II, or 70, 81, 87, 90 to Corso del Rinascimento

TRASTÈ (► 68)

CLUBS & DISCOS

ALIEN
Decor inspired by the film of the same name. An up-to-the-minute music policy has turned this futuristic club into one of Rome's nightspots of the moment.

➕ E4 ✉ Via Velletri 13–19 ☎ 06 841 2212 🕐 Tue–Sun 11PM–4AM 🚌 20N, 21N to Piazza Fiume 💶 Inexpensive to expensive (variable)

BLACK OUT
Regaining the reputation it won over a decade ago as one of the best alternative clubs. Music is mainly punk, thrash, Gothic—"dark" in Roman parlance.

➕ F7–F8 ✉ Via Saturnia 18 ☎ 06 7049 6791 🕐 Thu–Sat 10:30PM–4AM 🚇 Re di Roma 🚌 55N and 4, 87, 673 to Piazza Tuscolo 💶 Inexpensive to moderate (variable)

CARUSO
An established Latin and tropical dance venue, with live bands on Thursday nights. Also hip-hop and other styles depending on the evening.

➕ D8 ✉ Via Monte Testaccio 36 ☎ 06 574 5019 🕐 Mon–Sat 10:30PM–3AM 🚇 Piramide 🚌 13, 23, 27, 57, 95 💶 Membership moderate

GILDA
Gilda's louche and languid atmosphere has been attracting stars, VIPs, and wanna-be socialites for years. Bar, two stylish restaurants, glittering dance floor. Note that men are required to wear a smart jacket.

➕ fl; D5 ✉ Via Mario de' Fiori 97 ☎ 06 678 4838 🕐 Tue–Sun 11PM–4AM 🚇 Spagna 🚌 52, 53, 58, 61, 71, 85, 160 to Piazza San Silvestro 💶 Expensive

L'ALIBI
Primarily a gay disco, but not exclusively, L'Alibi is one of the most reliable (and most established) clubs now mushrooming in newly trendy Testaccio.

➕ D8 ✉ Via Monte Testaccio 40–44 ☎ 06 574 3448 🕐 Wed–Sun 11PM–4:30AM 🚇 Piramide 🚌 11, 13, 23, 27, 30, 57, 718 to Piazza di Porta San Paolo 💶 Moderate (free Sun, Thu)

PIPER
Open since the 1960s, Piper is consistently popular, thanks partly to its program of constant updating and refurbishment.

🕐 F3 ✉ Via Tagliamento 9 ☎ 06 855 5398/8046 🕐 Wed–Sat 10PM–5AM; Sun 3:30–7PM, 10PM–5AM 🚌 6N, 56, 57, 319 to Via Tagliamento 💶 Very expensive

THE SAINT
Three large, linked dance venues at the heart of the Testaccio nightlife district. The decor is currently inspired by the baroque era and by Dante: look out for the rooms labeled Inferno and Paradiso. Occasional live music.

➕ D8 ✉ Via Galvani 46 ☎ 06 574 7945 🕐 Mon–Sat 10:30PM–4AM 🚇 Piramide 🚌 13, 23, 27, 57, 95 💶 Inexpensive to expensive, depending on event

Membership and admission

Many Roman nightclubs and discos are run as private clubs (Associazioni Culturali), usually to circumvent planning or licensing laws. In practice this generally only means you have to buy a "membership card" (*una tessera*) in addition to the usual admission fee. The latter are high for the stylish places—mainly because Romans drink modestly and so clubs make little on their bar takings (admission usually includes a free first drink).

OPERA & CLASSICAL MUSIC

Church music

Following a decree from Pope John Paul II, all concert programs in Roman churches currently have a marked religious bias. Music can range from small-scale organ recitals to full-blown choirs and orchestras. Be on the lookout for posters advertising concerts outside churches and around the city. The Coro della Cappella Giulia sings at 10:30AM and 5PM on Sundays in St. Peter's. Sant'Ignazio di Loyola, San Paolo entro le Mura, San Nicola in Carcere, San Marcello al Corso, and Santa Maria dell'Orto are churches that regularly host choral and organ recitals.

ACCADEMIA FILARMONICA ROMANA

Founded in 1821, the Roman Philharmonic Academy numbers Rossini, Verdi and Donizetti among its distinguished early luminaries. Although it does not support its own choir or orchestra, it presents high-quality recitals of contemporary, choral, and symphonic music by well-known national and international performers. Concerts are held at either the Sala Casella (details as below) or the nearby Teatro Olimpico (► 81).

➕ C2 ✉ Via Flaminia 118
☎ 06 320 1752
🎵 Concerts Mid-Oct to mid-May Thu, occasionally Tue
Box office Daily 9AM–1PM, 6–7PM
Information Daily 3–7PM
🚌 225, 910 to Piazza Antonio Mancini

ACCADEMIA INTERNAZIONALE DI MUSICA

Usually arranges solo recitals and chamber concerts between November and June at the Sala Accademia northeast of the Villa Torlonia.

➕ G3 ✉ Via Giuseppe Antonio Guattani 17 ☎ 06 4425 2303
🚇 Bologna 🚌 36, 37, 60, 136, 137 to Via Nomentana

ACCADEMIA NAZIONALE DI SANTA CECILIA

In existence since the 16th century, Rome's main classical music body stages concerts by its own orchestra and choir, and organizes recitals and concerts by visiting choirs and orchestras. Most events are held at the Auditorio Pio, also known as the Auditorio di Santa Cecilia (below). Outdoor recitals and ballet performances are held in July at the Villa Giulia (► 35).

➕ f1; D4 ✉ Via Vittoria 6
☎ 06 678 0742
Villa Giulia concert information
☎ 06 361 1064

ACQUARIO ROMANO

An innovative organization whose concerts showcase contemporary classical music—both well-known and, occasionally, obscure.

➕ F6 ✉ Piazza Manfredo Fanti 47 ☎ 06 446 8616 or 06 6880 9222 🚇 Termini or Vittorio Emanuele 🚌 4, 9, 70, 71

AUDITORIO DEL FORO ITALICO

Rome's premier state-owned auditorium is part of the Mussolini-era sports city in the northwest. It is home to the orchestra of RAI, the national radio and television company.

➕ B2 ✉ Piazza Lauro De Bossis ☎ 06 3686 5625
🎵 Concerts Nov–Jun: Fri 6:30PM. Oct: Fri 6:30PM; Sat 9PM
Box office Thu–Sat 10–1, 4–7
🚌 32, 186, 280, 291, 391 to Lungotevere Maresciallo Cadorna

AUDITORIO PIO (AUDITORIO DI SANTA CECILIA)

➕ cl1; B5 ✉ Via della Conciliazione 4
Box office ☎ 06 6880 1044 (credit cards ☎ 06 3938 7297)
🎵 Mon–Fri 10:30–1:30, 3–6
🚌 64 to Piazza San Pietro, or 23, 34, 41, 46, 62, 65, 98, 280, 881 to Ponte Vittorio Emanuele II

AULA DEL PONTIFICIO ISTITUTO DI MUSICA SACRA

✚ ell; C5 ✉ Piazza Sant'Agostino 20a ☎ 06 678 9258 🚌 119 to Piazza Cinque Lune, or 70, 81, 87, 90, 186, 492 to Corso del Rinascimento

AULA MAGNA DELL'UNIVERSITÀ LA SAPIENZA

✚ G5 ✉ Piazzale Aldo Moro 5 ☎ 06 361 0052 🎫 Concerts Oct–May: Tue 8:30PM; Sat 5:30PM 🚌 9, 310 to Viale dell'Università

IL GONFALONE

The Gonfalone is a small but prestigious company that hosts chamber music and other small-scale recitals at its own Oratorio.

✚ dlll; C6 ✉ Oratorio del Gonfalone, Via del Gonfalone 32a **Information** ✉ Vicolo della Scimmia 1b ☎ 06 687 5952 🎫 Concerts Oct–Jun: Thu 9PM Box office Mon–Fri 9AM–1PM; day of concert 9AM–9PM 🚌 46, 62, 64 to Corso Vittorio Emanuele II, or 23, 41, 65, 280 to Lungotevere di Sangallo

INTERNATIONAL CHAMBER ENSEMBLE

Small body whose chamber and modest orchestral concerts usually take place in the Anglican All Saints' church.

✚ D4 ✉ Via del Babuino 153 ☎ 06 8680 0125 🚇 Spagna 🚌 119

ISTITUTO UNIVERSITARIO DEI CONCERTI (IUC)

The IUC students keep the music exciting and eclectic. Concert cycles are devoted to the music and composers of a different country each year. Most recitals are in the university's Aula Magna just east of Stazione Termini.

✚ B2 ✉ Lungotevere Flaminio 50 ☎ 06 361 0051/0052 🎫 **Box office** Mon–Fri 10AM–1PM, 3–6PM; Sat 10AM–1PM 🚌 225, 910 to Piazza Mancini

TEATRO DELL'OPERA

Rome's opera house is enduring lean times. Crippled by mismanagement and dwindling finances, the reputation of its orchestra and choir and the quality and range of performances has diminished. Austerity has forced a concentration on the mainstream repertoire. Between mid-June and mid-August operas are staged outdoors at the Piazza di Siena in the Villa Borghese.

✚ hll; E5 🎭 **Opera** Piazza Beniamo Gigli ☎ 06 481 7003 (or, toll-free in Italy ☎ 167 016665) **Box office** ✉ Via Firenze 72 ☎ 06 481601 🎭 **Opera** Mid-Jun to mid-Aug, Dec–May **Recitals** Nov–Jun 🚇 Termini 🚌 57, 64, 65, 70, 71, 75, 170 to Via Nazionale, or services to Termini

TEATRO OLIMPICO

✚ C2 ✉ Piazza Gentile da Fabriano ☎ 06 323 4890 **Box office** ☎ 06 323 4936 (credit cards ☎ 06 3938 2747) 🎫 daily 11–7 🚌 225, 280, 301, 910 to Piazza Mancini

Music outdoors

Alfresco recitals often take place in the cloisters of Santa Maria della Pace in July (part of the Serenate in Chiostro season); in the Villa Doria Pamphili in July (as part of the the Festival Villa Pamphili); in the grounds of the Villa Giulia in the summer (as part of the Stagione Estivi dell'Orchestra dell'Accademia di Santa Cecilia); and in the Area Archeologica del Teatro di Marcello from July to September (as part of the Estate al Tempietto, also known as the Concerti del Tempietto). Note that the venues may change from year to year.

LIVE MUSIC

Listings and tickets

For details of upcoming events, consult the listings magazine *roma c'è*, available from most newsstands, or the free *Trovaroma* listings supplement published with the Thursday edition of *La Repubblica*. Otherwise, see the daily listings of *Il Messaggero*. Tickets for events can be bought at the door, or from the following agencies:

Orbis ✉ Piazza Esquilino 37 ☎ 06 482 7403 🕐 Mon–Sat 9:30–1, 4–7:30

Box Office ✉ Via Giulio Cesare 88 ☎ 06 372 0216 🕐 Mon 3:30–7; Tue–Sat 10–1, 2:30–7 ✉ Via del Corso 506 ☎ 06 361 2682 🕐 Mon 3:30–7; Tue–Sat 10–1, 2:30–7

Note that credit cards are not accepted at either agency. Tickets are also available from the Ricordi music store (✉ Via del Corso 506 ☎ 06 361 2331).

As with clubs and discos (► 79), you may need to buy an annual membership card (*una tessera*) on top of a ticket for a music venue. Virtually all clubs close between late July and early September.

ALEXANDERPLATZ

A restaurant and cocktail bar north of St. Peter's with live jazz.
🚑 B4 ✉ Via Ostia 9 ☎ 06 3974 2171 🕐 Sep–Jun: Mon–Sat 9–2 🚇 Ottaviano 🚌 29N, 30N, 99N, and 23, 70, 291, 490, 913, 991, 994, 999 to Largo Trionfale-Viale delle Milizie 🎫 Four-month membership (expensive); free to tourists on production of passport

BERIMBAU

Brazilian club with live music, powerful cocktails, and a multi-ethnic audience. Bands usually followed by disco sessions.
🚑 eIV ✉ Via dei Fienaroli 30b ☎ 06 581 3249 🕐 Wed–Sun 11:30PM–3AM 🚌 Tue, Sun inexpensive; Fri, Sat moderate (admission includes a drink)

BIG MAMA

Rome's best blues club; also hosts rock and jazz.
🚑 C4 ✉ Vicolo San Francesco a Ripa 18 ☎ 06 581 2551 🕐 Oct–Jun: daily 9PM–1:30AM 🚌 13, 44, 75, 170, 181, 280, 717 to Viale di Trastevere 🎫 Yearly membership (moderate) plus fee for some concerts

CAFFÈ LATINO

The oldest club in Testaccio, devoted to eating, drinking, live music, and dance sessions. Mostly jazz, but rap, blues, and other genres are represented.
🚑 D8 ✉ Via Monte Testaccio 96 ☎ 06 5728 8384 🕐 Sep–Jul: Tue–Thu, Sun 10:30PM– 2:30AM; Fri, Sat 10:30PM–4:30AM 🚇 Piramide 🚌 13, 23, 27, 57, 95 to Via Marmorata 🎫 Annual membership (expensive)

FOLKSTUDIO

This laid-back folk and blues venue, which opened in the 1960s, presents top Italian and international talent.
🚑 hIII; E6 ✉ Via Frangipane 42 ☎ 06 487 1063 🕐 Mid-Sep to early Jun: daily 9:30PM–12 🚌 N20, N21 and 11, 27, 81, 85, 87, 186 to Via dei Fori Imperiali 🚇 Colosseo 🎫 Yearly membership (moderate) plus entry (expensive)

FONCLEA

Jazz predominates at this bar, restaurant, and club close to St. Peter's.
🚑 B5–C5 ✉ Via Crescenzio 82a ☎ 06 689 6302 🕐 Mon–Thu, Sun 8PM–2AM; Fri, Sat 9PM–3AM 🚌 29N, 30N and 23, 34, 49, 492, 990 to Via Crescenzio 🎫 Free (except Sat: inexpensive)

JAM SESSION MUSIC

Popular modern jazz, soul, R&B, and fusion in an underground joint.
🚑 hIV; E6 ✉ Via del Cardello 13a ☎ 06 474 5076 🕐 Wed–Sun 8:30PM–3AM 🚇 Colosseo or Cavour 🚌 20N, 21N and 11, 27, 81, 85, 87, 186 to Via Cavour-Via dei Fori Imperiali 🎫 Three-month membership (expensive)

MISSISSIPPI JAZZ CLUB

Re-creates the feel of an American jazz dive with period photos of past performers. The biggest names play on Friday and Saturday. Food available.
🚑 bI–cI; B5 ✉ Borgo Angelico 18a ☎ 06 6880 6348 🕐 Daily 9:30PM–2AM 🎫 Membership (inexpensive)

SPORTS

ACQUA ACETOSA

Public sports facilities also
used for rugby games and
swimming tournaments.
🏳 E1 ✉ Via dei Campi Sportivi
48 ☎ 06 36851 🕐 Daily
9AM–7:30PM 🚇 Acqua Acetosa or
Campi Sportivi 🚌 4, 391

HORSE RACING

IPPODROMO DELLE CAPANNELLE

Rome's main race course
hosts flat racing,
steeplechasing, and
trotting.
✉ Via Appia Nuova 1255
☎ 06 718 3143 🕐 Races
Sep–Jun: Mon, Wed, Fri, Sun
1:30–7:30PM 🚌 650, 671 to
Via Appia Nuova

SOCCER

STADIO OLIMPICO

Rome's two big soccer
teams, AS Roma and
Lazio, play their home
games here on alternate
Sundays.
🏳 B1 ✉ Viale dei Gladiatori
☎ 06 3685 7520
Ticket office
☎ 06 323 7333
🕐 Daily 9–1:30, 2:30–6
AS Roma information
☎ 06 506 0200
Lazio information
☎ 06 3685 7566/06 323 7465
🚌 32, 186, 280, 291, 391 to
Lungotevere Maresciallo Cadorna

SPECTATOR SPORTS

FORO ITALICO

One of the world's finest
sports stadia when built in
the 1930s, the Foro Italico
is today best known as the
site of the Italian open
tennis tournament in May.
🏳 B2 ✉ Lungotevere

Maresciallo Diaz-Viale dei
Gladiatori 31 ☎ 06 36851/333
6316 🚌 32, 186, 280, 291, 391
to Lungotevere Maresciallo
Cadorna

PALAZZETTO DELLO SPORT

Part of the EUR complex
built for the 1960 Olympic
Games. Hosts boxing,
fencing, tennis, and
wrestling.
🏳 C2 ✉ Piazza Apollodoro-Via
Flaminia 🕐 Daily 7AM–8PM
🚇 Flaminio 🚌 225, 910 to
Piazza Apollodoro

PALAZZO DELLO SPORT

Another part of the EUR
complex, this stadium
hosts indoor games, most
notably basketball every
Sunday at 5:30pm.
🏳 C13 ✉ Via dell'Umanesimo
☎ 06 592 5006/6809/5107
🚇 EUR Palasport

SWIMMING

Public swimming pools in
Rome are either some way
from the center or not
terribly pleasant. Your best
option is to use a hotel
pool; many open to
nonresidents for a daily
fee. Two of the best are at
the Aldrovandi Palace and
Cavalieri Hilton.
Aldrovandi Palace 🏳 D3
✉ Via Ulisse Aldrovandi 15
☎ 06 322 3993 🕐 Jun–Sep:
daily 10–6 🚌 19, 30 to Via
Aldrovandi
Cavalieri Hilton 🏳 E3
✉ Via Alberto Cadlolo 101
☎ 06 35091 🚌 907, 913,
991, 999 to Via Medaglie d'Oro

Local rivalry

Rivalry between Rome's two
Serie A (first division) soccer teams
is intense. Lazio, a traditional
underachiever, is currently doing
as well as AS Roma, once among
Italy's soccer elite (its last
championship, or *scudetto*, was in
1982–83). AS Roma is known as
the *giallorossi* (after the team's red
and yellow uniform), while Lazio
players sport the nickname
biancocelesti, referring to their
colors, white and sky blue.
The team symbols—AS Roma's
wolf cub and Lazio's eagle—are
often seen among city graffiti.

LUXURY HOTELS

Hotel prices

Expect to pay the following prices per night for a double room, but it's always worth asking when you make your reservation whether any special deals are available.

Budget   up to L150,000
Mid-range   up to L300,000
Luxury   from L300,000

Reservations

Rome's peak season runs from Easter to October, but the city's hotels (in all categories) are almost invariably busy. Telephone, write, or fax well in advance to reserve a room (most receptionists speak some English, French, or German). Leave a credit card number or send an international money order for the first night's stay to be certain of the booking. Reconfirm a few days before your trip. If you arrive without a reservation, get to a hotel early in the morning; by afternoon most vacated rooms will have been snapped up. Don't accept rooms from touts at Stazione Termini.

ALBERGO DEL SOLE AL PANTHEON

Chic and old—open since 1467. Opposite the Pantheon; if you can stand the crowds, the location is one of the best.

➕ ell; D5 ✉ Piazza della Rotonda 63 ☎ 06 678 0441 🚌 119 to Piazza della Rotonda, or 70, 81, 87, 90 to Corso del Rinascimento

AMBASCIATORI PALACE

One of the more venerable and stately of the Via Veneto's large luxury hotels, with a traditional feel and opulent appearance.

➕ gl; E5 ✉ Via Vittorio Veneto 62 ☎ 06 47493 🚇 Barberini 🚌 52, 53, 56, 58, 95 to Via Vittorio Veneto

EXCELSIOR

One of the largest and grandest. Everything is on an enormous scale, from the vast silk rugs to the palatial bedrooms.

➕ gl; E5 ✉ Via Vittorio Veneto 125 ☎ 06 47081 🚇 Barberini 🚌 52, 53, 56, 58, 95 to Via Vittorio Veneto

HASSLER-VILLA MEDICI

Famous, magnificently situated longtime jet set and VIP haunt, just above the Spanish Steps.

➕ fl; D5 ✉ Piazza Trinità dei Monti 6 ☎ 06 699340 🚇 Spagna 🚌 119 to Piazza di Spagna

HOLIDAY INN CROWNE PLAZA MINERVA ROME

Well-designed hotel in the shadow of the Pantheon and Santa Maria sopra Minerva.

➕ fIII; D5 ✉ Piazza della Minerva 69 ☎ 06 6994 1888 🚌 119 to Piazza della Rotonda, 70, 81, 87, 90 to Corso del Rinascimento

INGHILTERRA

Founded in 1850, and host to such guests as Liszt and Hemingway, this club-like hotel is near the best shopping streets.

➕ fl; D5 ✉ Via Bocca di Leone 14 ☎ 06 69981 🚇 Spagna 🚌 119 to Piazza di Spagna, or 52, 53, 58, 61, 71, 85, 160 to Piazza San Silvestro

LE GRAND HOTEL

Not in the most salubrious location, but immensely lavish and often rated the city's most luxurious.

➕ hl; E5 ✉ Via Vittorio Emanuele Orlando 3 ☎ 06 47091/474709 🚇 Repubblica 🚌 57, 64, 65, 75, 170, 492, 910 to Piazza della Repubblica

LORD BYRON

Small, refined, and extremely chic, away from the center in leafy Parioli. Noted for its excellent restaurant, Relais Le Jardin.

➕ D3 ✉ Via Giuseppe de Notaris 5 ☎ 06 322 0404 🚇 Flaminio 🚌 52, 926 to Via Buozzi

RAPHAEL

Intimate, charming, and ivy-covered; hidden away yet near Piazza Navona. Rooms are a little small, but the furniture and fixtures are immaculate. Reserve ahead.

➕ ell; C5 ✉ Largo Febo 2 ☎ 06 682831 🚌 70, 81, 87, 90 to Corso del Rinascimento

MID-RANGE HOTELS

CAMPO DE' FIORI
Good value, near Campo de' Fiori. Rooms are small but pretty, and there is a roof garden.
✚ elll; C6 ⊠ Via del Biscione 6 ☎ 06 6880 6865 ▣ 46, 62, 64 to Corso Vittorio Emanuele II

CESARI
A thoroughly reliable, friendly and no-frills hotel with a loyal clientele. Perfectly located between the Corso and the Pantheon.
✚ flll; D5 ⊠ Via di Pietra 89a ☎ 06 679 2386 ▣ 56, 60, 62, 85, 90, 160 to Via del Corso

COLUMBUS
A converted monastery just a minute's walk from St. Peter's. A favorite with visiting cardinals.
✚ cll; B5 ⊠ Via della Conciliazione 33 ☎ 06 686 5435 ▣ 23, 24 to Via della Conciliazione or 64 to Piazza San Pietro

DUE TORRI
Hidden in a tiny alley between Piazza Navona and the Tiber. Rooms vary from stylish to plain, but all are adequate.
✚ ell; C5 ⊠ Vicolo del Leonetto 23–5 ☎ 06 6880 6956 ▣ 70, 81, 87, 90, 186 to Corso del Rinascimento or Lungotevere Marzio

HOTEL PORTOGHESI
A well-known if slightly fading hotel with a roof terrace. Located in a cobbled street just north of Sant'Agostino and Piazza Navona.
✚ ell; C5 ⊠ Via dei Portoghesi 1 ☎ 06 686 4231 ▣ 70, 81, 87, 90 to Corso del Rinascimento

LA RESIDENZA
A good choice: near Via Vittorio Veneto and reasonably priced. Stylish public spaces, spacious, and comfortable rooms. Terrace and roof garden.
✚ E4 ⊠ Via Emilia 22–4 ☎ 06 488 0789 🚇 Barberini ▣ 52, 53, 56, 58, 95 to Via Vittorio Veneto

LOCARNO
In a quietish side street near Piazza del Popolo. Much genuine 1920s art nouveau decor.
✚ C4 ⊠ Via della Penna 22 ☎ 06 361 0841 🚇 Flaminio ▣ 90, 119, 926 to Via di Ripetta, or 81 to Lungotevere in Augusta

MANFREDI
Small, family-run hotel in a cobbled street of galleries and antique shops. Pretty and quiet.
✚ D4 ⊠ Via Margutta 61 ☎ 06 320 7676 🚇 Spagna ▣ 119 to Piazza di Spagna

MARGUTTA
Rooms are bright, quaint, and comfortable, although the public areas are a little spartan. Near Piazza del Popolo.
✚ D4 ⊠ Via Laurina 34 ☎ 06 322 3674 🚇 Spagna ▣ 119 to Piazza di Spagna

SISTINA
Small, reliable, efficient, and close to the Piazza di Spagna. Lovely terrace for drinks and breakfasts.
✚ gl; D5 ⊠ Via Sistina 136 ☎ 06 474 5000 🚇 Spagna or Barberini ▣ 119 to Piazza di Spagna, or 52, 53, 56, 58, 60, 61, 62 to Piazza Barberini

Prices
Hotels are classified by the Italian state into five categories from one star (basic) to five stars (luxury). The prices each can charge are set by law and must be displayed in the room (you will usually find them on the door). However, prices within a hotel can vary from room to room (and some hotels have off- and peak-season rates). If a room is too expensive, do not be afraid to ask for a cheaper one. Watch for extras like air-conditioning and obligatory breakfasts. Single rooms cost about two-thirds the price of doubles, and to have an extra bed in a room adds 35 percent to the check.

85

BUDGET ACCOMMODATIONS

Noise

Noise is a fact of life in every Roman hotel, whatever the price category. Surveys have shown Rome to be the noisiest city in Europe. You will never escape the cacophony entirely (unless the hotel is air-conditioned and windows are double-glazed), but to lessen the potential racket you should avoid rooms overlooking main thoroughfares and the area around Termini in favor of rooms looking out on parks or obscure back streets. Also ask for rooms away from the front of the hotel or facing on to a central courtyard (*cortile*).

ABRUZZI

Twenty-five large, basic rooms (and eight shared bathrooms), some with a view of the Pantheon (noisy); rooms at the rear are quieter.

➕ ell; D5 ✉ Piazza della Rotonda 69 ☎ 06 679 2021 🚌 119 to Piazza della Rotonda, or 44, 46, 75, 87, 94, 170 to Largo di Torre Argentina

FIORELLA

Eight bright, airy, and spotless rooms (two shared bathrooms) in a part of town with few budget-priced hotels. 1AM curfew.

➕ D4 ✉ Via del Babuino 196 ☎ 06 361 0597 🚇 Spagna 🚌 119 to Piazza di Spagna

KATTY

Less grim than most of the countless cheap hotels in the unsavory area near Rome's main train station, and its 18 rooms are always reserved in advance.

➕ F5 ✉ Via Palestro 5 ☎ 06 444 1216 🚇 Termini 🚌 27, 64, 65, 170 and all other services to Termini

NAVONA

Twenty-six simple rooms, friendly owners, and a superb central location (just west of Piazza Sant'Eustacchio). Reserve well in advance.

➕ ell; C5 ✉ Via dei Sediari 8 ☎ 06 686 4203 🚌 70, 81, 87, 90, 186, 492 to Corso del Rinascimento

PERUGIA

Little-known, quiet and well located between Via Cavour and the Colosseum. All eight doubles have private bathrooms.

➕ hIV; E6 ✉ Via del Colosseo 7 ☎ 06 679 7200 🚌 11, 27, 81 to Via Cavour, or 85, 87, 186 to the Colosseum

PICCOLO

Fine little hotel near Campo de' Fiori. Only half of the 16 rooms have private bathrooms.

➕ C6 ✉ Via dei Chiavari 32 ☎ 06 6880 2560/06 689 2330 🚌 46, 62, 64 to Corso Vittorio Emanuele II, or 44, 56, 60, 65, 75, 170 to Via Arenula

POMEZIA

The 22 rooms are small (11 have private bathrooms), but the location near Campo de' Fiori is central. Roof terrace and small bar.

➕ ell; C6 ✉ Via dei Chiavari 12 ☎ 06 686 1371 🚌 46, 62, 64 to Corso Vittorio Emanuele II, or 44, 56, 60, 65, 75, 170 to Via Arenula

SMERALDO

Plain, clean, and straightforward. In a back street a couple of minutes' walk from Campo de' Fiori.

➕ elll; C6 ✉ Vicolo dei Chiodaroli 11 ☎ 06 687 5929 🚌 46, 62, 64 to Corso Vittorio Emanuele II, or 44, 56, 60, 65, 75, 170 to Via Arenula

SOLE

A popular budget choice, on the edge of Campo de' Fiori. There are 62 rooms, but it is essential to reserve. Small garden terrace.

➕ elll; C6 ✉ Via del Biscione 76 ☎ 06 6880 6873/5258 🚌 46, 62, 64 to Corso Vittorio Emanuele II, or 44, 56, 60, 65, 75, 170 to Via Arenula

ROME
travel facts

Arriving & Departing

Before you go

- All visitors to Italy require a valid passport.
- Visas are not required for U.S., Canadian, Australian, New Zealand, U.K. or Irish citizens, or for other E.U. nationals staying under three months.
- Vaccinations are not required unless you are coming from a known infected area.

Travel insurance

- Take out full health and travel insurance before traveling to Italy.

When to go

- January and February are the quietest months.
- April to early June and mid-September to October are best.
- Easter Week is busy.
- Many restaurants and businesses close for a month in August.

Climate

- Winters are short and cold.
- Spring begins in March; April and May can be muggy and rainy.
- Summers are hot and dry, with sudden thunderstorms. July and August are uncomfortably hot.
- Weather in autumn is mixed, but can produce crisp days with clear skies.

Arriving by air

- Scheduled flights arrive at Leonardo da Vinci airport, better known as Fiumicino. Inquiries ☎ 06 6595 3640/3088
- Shuttle trains link Fiumicino to Stazione Termini in the city center. Inquiries ☎ 06 4775
- Taxis are slow and expensive. Take only licensed (white or yellow) cabs or a pre-paid "car with driver" available from the SOCAT desk in the International Arrivals hall.
- Charter flights use Ciampino, a military airport south of Rome. Information ☎ 06 794941
- From Ciampino go by COTRAL bus to Anagnina or Subaugusta, and then by Metro line A to Stazione Termini.

Arriving by train

- Most trains arrive and depart from Stazione Termini, which is well placed for most of central Rome.
- Taxis and buses leave from the station forecourt, Piazza dei Cinquecento.
- Train information ☎ 147 888088 (toll-free) 🕐 daily 7AM–9PM

Customs regulations

- Duty-free limits for non-E.U. visitors are: 400 cigarettes or 200 small cigars or 500g of tobacco; 1 liter of spirits (over 22 percent alcohol) or 2 liters of fortified wine (over 22 percent alcohol); 50g of perfume.

Essential Facts

Tourist information

- Ente Provinciale per il Turismo di Roma ✉ Via Parigi 11 ☎ 06 488 991 🕐 Mon–Fri 8:15AM–7:15PM
- Tourist information kiosks can be found at:

✉ Largo Goldoni	☎ 06 6813 6061
✉ Fori Imperiali	☎ 06 6992 4307
✉ Piazza delle Cinque Lune	☎ 06 6880 9240
✉ Via Nazionale	☎ 06 4782 4525
✉ La Rinascente, Via del Tritone	☎ 06 6920 0435
✉ Piazza San Giovanni in Laterano	☎ 06 7720 3598
✉ Lungotevere Castel Sant'Angelo-Piazza Pia	☎ 06 6880 9707

Opening hours

- Stores: Tue–Sat 8–1, 4–8; Mon 4–8 (with slight seasonal variations). Food shops open on Monday mornings but usually close on Thursday afternoons.
- Restaurants: daily 12:30–3, 7:30–10:30. Many close on Sunday evenings and half- or all day Monday. Most bars and restaurants also have a statutory closing day (*riposo settimanale*) and many close for much of August.
- Churches: variable, but usually daily 7–noon, 4:30–7.
- Museums and galleries: vary considerably; usually close on Monday.
- Banks: Mon–Fri 8:30–1:30. Major branches may also open 3–4 and Saturday morning.
- Post offices: Mon–Fri 8:15 or 9–2; Sat 8:15 or 9–noon or 2.

Public holidays

- Jan 1:   New Year's Day;
- Jan 6:   Epiphany;
- Easter Monday;
- Apr 25:   National holiday;
- May 1:   Labor Day;
- Jun 29:   SS Peter & Paul's Day;
- Aug 15:   Assumption;
- Nov 1:   All Saints' Day;
- Dec 8:   Immaculate Conception;
- Dec 25:   Christmas Day;
- Dec 26:   St. Stephen's Day.

Money matters

- The Italian currency is the lira, abbreviated to "L."
- Notes: L1,000, L2,000, L5,000, L10,000, L50,000, and L100,000.
- Coins: L5 and L10 (both rare), L50, L100, L200, L500, and a new L1,000, plus a L200 telephone token (*gettone*) which can be used as a coin.
- Most major traveler's checks can be changed at banks, though lines can be long.

- Credit cards (*carte di credito*) are gaining in popularity, but cash is preferred. ATMs are not as common as in the United States.

Women travelers

- Expect some hassles (rarely threatening) from Italian men.
- At night avoid the parks and the area around Termini.

Time differences

- Italy is six hours ahead of New York and nine hours ahead of Los Angeles.

Electricity

- Current is 220 volts AC, 50 cycles; plugs are the two-round-pin type.

Etiquette

- Do not wear shorts, short skirts, or skimpy tops in churches.
- Avoid entering churches while services are in progress.
- Many churches and galleries forbid flash photography, or ban photography altogether. Always ask before taking pictures.
- Smoking is common in bars and restaurants, but is banned on public transport.
- Public drunkenness is rare and frowned upon. Public displays of affection, however, are the norm!

PUBLIC TRANSPORTATION

Buses and trams

- Rome's orange buses and trams, run by ATAC, have cheap and frequent services.
- Blue regional and suburban buses are run by COTRAL.
- Buses are often crowded and the traffic slow.
- ATAC information ➕ F5 ✉ Piazza dei Cinquecento ☎ 167 431784 (toll-free) 🕐 Mon–Fri 9–1, 2–5 🚇 Termini

- Buy tickets before boarding the bus; they are available from automatic machines, shops and newsstands displaying an ATAC sticker, and tobacconists (indicated by signs showing a white "T" on a blue background).
- Your bus ticket (called a "BIT") must be stamped at the rear of the bus or tram, and is valid for any number of bus rides and one Metro ride within a 75-minute time period. Remember to enter buses by back doors and to leave by center doors (if you have a pass or validated ticket with unexpired time you can also use the front doors).
- Buy several tickets at once as some outlets close early.
- There are L50,000 fines if you are caught without a ticket.
- Daytime services: 5:30AM–11:30PM, depending on the route. Bus stops (*fermate*) list routes and bus numbers. Note that one-way streets often force buses to return along slightly different routes.
- Night service (*servizio notturno*): 30 buses run on key routes from about midnight to 5:30AM. Unlike day buses they have a conductor who sells tickets.
- Useful services:
  23 Piazza del Risorgimento (for the Vatican Museums)–Trastevere–Piramide.
  27 Termini–Roman Forum–Colosseum–Piramide.
  46 Piazza Venezia–Vatican.
  56, **60** and **75** Piazza Venezia–Trastevere.
  64 Stazione Termini–Piazza Venezia–Corso Vittorio Emanuele II–St. Peter's.
  81 Piazza del Risorgimento (Vatican Museums)–Via Nazionale–Roman Forum–Colosseum–San Giovanni in Laterano.

119 Circular minibus service in the historic center: Piazza Augusto Imperatore–Piazza della Rotonda (Pantheon)–Via del Corso–Piazza di Spagna.

Metro

- Rome's subway system (*la Metropolitana*, or *Metro*) has just two lines—named A and B—which intersect at Stazione Termini. Primarily a commuter service, it is of only limited use in the city center. It is good, however, for quick trans-city rides.
- Stations at Colosseo, Spagna, Barberini, Repubblica, Termini, and San Giovanni are convenient to major sights.
- Station entrances are marked by a large red M, and each has a map of the network.
- Tickets are valid for one ride and can be bought from tobacconists (*tabacchi*), bars, and shops displaying ATAC or COTRAL stickers, and—if they are working—from machines at stations (exact change only). Day passes are also available.
- Services: daily 5:30AM–11:30PM except Sat 5:30AM–12:30PM.

Passes

- An integrated ticket, the *Biglietto Integrato* (BIG) is available from the sources listed above. It is valid for a day's unlimited travel on ATAC buses, the Metro, COTRAL buses and suburban railroads (except to Fiumicino airport).
- Weekly passes (*Carta Integrata Settimanale*) are valid for a week; services as for BIG tickets.

Taxis

- Licensed taxis: official Rome taxis are yellow or white, with a "Taxi" sign on the roof. Use only these and refuse offers from touts at

Fiumicino, Termini, and elsewhere.

- Calling a cab: the firm will give you a taxi code name, a number, and the time it will take to get to you. The meter starts running as soon as they are called.
  Firms include:
  Cosmos Radio Taxis ☎ 06 88177
  Autoradio Taxi ☎ 06 3570
  Capitale Radio ☎ 06 4994

- When hailing a cab make sure the meter is set at zero. The minimum fare is valid for 3km or the first 9 minutes of a ride. Surcharges are levied between 10PM and 7AM, all day Sunday, on public holidays, for airport trips, and for each piece of luggage in the trunk.

- Drivers are not supposed to stop on the streets (though some do), and it is therefore difficult to hail a passing cab. Taxis congregate at stands, indicated by blue signs with *Taxi* printed on them in white. Stands can be found downtown at Termini, Piazza Venezia, Largo Argentina, Piazza S. Sonnino, Pantheon, Piazza di Spagna, and Piazza San Silvestro.

MEDIA & COMMUNICATIONS

Telephones

- Telephone numbers listed in this book include the Rome area code (06), which must be dialed even if you are calling from within the city.

- Public telephones are indicated by a red or yellow sign showing a telephone dial and receiver. They are found on the street, in bars, and restaurants, and in special offices (*Centri Telefoni*) equipped with banks of phones and (occasionally) staff.

- A few *Centri Telefoni* have phones that allow you to speak first and pay later, but most phones at booths require prepayment.

- Phones accept L100, L200, and L500 coins, L200 tokens known as *gettoni*, and, usually, phone cards (*schede telefoniche*, available from post offices, tobacco stores, and some bars in L5,000, L10,000 and L15,000 denominations). Break off the card's small marked corner before use.

- Cheap rate for calls is Mon–Sat 10PM–8AM and all day Sunday.

- To call Italy from the United States or Canada, dial 011 followed by 39 (the country code for Italy) then the number, including the relevant city code. For example, to call the main tourist office in Rome dial: 011 39 06 488911.

Postal service

- Stamps (*francobolli*) can be bought from post offices and most tobacco stores.

- Post boxes are red and have two slots, one for Rome (marked *Per La Città*) and one for other destinations (*Per Tutte Le Altre Destinazioni*).

- Vatican mail can be posted only in the Vatican's blue *Poste Vaticane* mail boxes. The Vatican postal service is quicker (although tariffs are the same), but stamps can be bought only at the post offices in the Vatican Museums ⊚ Mon–Fri 8:30AM–7PM and in Piazza San Pietro ☎ 06 6982 ⊚ Mon–Fri 8:30AM–7PM; Sat 8:30AM–6PM.

- Most post offices (*Posta* or *Ufficio Postale*) open Mon–Fri 8:15AM–2:30PM; Sat and the last day of each month 8:15AM–noon. The main post office, the *Ufficio Postale Centrale*, is at Piazza San Silvestro 18–20 ☎ 06 6771 and usually opens Mon–Fri 8:30AM–7:40PM; Sat 8:30AM–noon.

Newspapers and magazines

- Most Romans read the Rome-based *Il Messaggero*, the mainstream and authoritative *Corriere della Sera*, or the center-left and popularist *La Repubblica* (which has a special Rome edition). Sports papers and news magazines (like *Panorama* and *L'Espresso*) are also popular.
- Foreign newspapers can usually be bought after about 2:30PM on the day of issue from booths (*edicole*) in and near Termini, Piazza Colonna, Largo di Torre Argentina, Piazza Navona, Via Vittoria Veneto, and close to several other tourist sights. European editions of the *International Herald Tribune, USA Today*, and the *Financial Times* are also available.

Radio and television

- Italian television is divided between the three channels of the state network RAI, the three private channels founded by Silvio Berlusconi (Canale 5, Rete 4, and Italia 1), and a host of smaller commercial stations.
- RAI also runs a public radio service, but the airwaves are dominated by smaller (mainly FM) stations.

EMERGENCIES

Safety

- Carry all valuables in a belt or pouch—never in your pocket.
- Hold bags across your front, never over one shoulder, where they can be grabbed or rifled.
- Wear your camera—never put it down on a café table.
- Leave valuables (especially chains and earrings) in the hotel safe.
- Beware of persistent small gangs of street children. If approached, hang on to possessions, raise your voice and, if necessary, push them away.

- Never leave luggage or other possessions in parked cars.
- Beware of pickpockets, especially in crowded tourist areas, busy shopping streets, and buses (the 64 bus to St. Peter's is notorious).
- Avoid parks and the back streets around Termini late at night.

Lost property

- To make a claim on lost or stolen property report the loss to a police station, which will issue a signed declaration (*una denuncia*) for your insurance company. The central police station is the Questura.
  ✉ Via San Vitale 15 (off Via Nazionale) ☎ 06 4686 (tourist department ☎ 06 4686 2102) Ⓜ Repubblica
- ATAC lost property
  ✉ Via Nicola Bettoni 1 ☎ 06 581 6040 🕐 Daily 9AM–noon
- Metro line A lost property
  ✉ Furio Camillo Metro Station ☎ 06 5753 3620 🕐 Mon, Tue, Fri 9AM–noon
- COTRAL lost property
  ✉ Inquire at the route's origin or telephone ☎ 06 57531/06 591 5551
- Railroad lost property
  ✉ Stazione Termini, Via Giovanni Giolitti 24 (near Platform 22) ☎ 06 4730 6682 🕐 Mon–Fri 7AM–10PM

Medical and dental treatment

- There are emergency rooms (*Pronto Soccorso*) at these centers: Ospedale Fatebenefratelli
  ✉ Isola Tiberina ☎ 06 58 731
  Policlinico Umberto
  ✉ Viale Policlinico ☎ 06 446 2341
  International Medical Center
  ✉ Via Giovanni Amendola 7 ☎ 06 488 2371
- The George Eastman Clinic provides an emergency dentist service. No credit cards.
  ✉ Viale Regina Elena 287 ☎ 06 844831
- Pharmacies are indicated by a large green cross. Opening times are usually Mon–Sat 8:30–1, 4–8, but a rotating schedule (displayed

on pharmacy doors) ensures at least one pharmacy is open 24 hours a day, seven days a week.
- The most central English-speaking pharmacist is Internazionale ✉ Piazza Barberini 49 ☎ 06 487 1195

Key telephone numbers
- Police, Fire and Ambulance (general SOS) ☎ 113
- Police (Carabinieri) ☎ 112
- Central Police ☎ 06 4686
- US Embassy ☎ 06 46741
- Information ☎ 12
- International information (Europe) ☎ 15
- International information (rest of the world) ☎ 170
- ACI Auto Assistance (car breakdowns) ☎ 116

LANGUAGE

- Italians respond well to foreigners who make an effort to speak their language (however badly). Many Italians speak some English, and most upscale hotels and restaurants have multilingual staff.
- All Italian words are pronounced as written, with each vowel and consonant sounded. Only the letter *h* is silent, but it modifies the sound of other letters. The letter *c* is hard, as in English "cat," except when followed by *i* or *e*, when it becomes the soft *ch* of "cello." Similarly, *g* is soft (as in the English "giant") when followed by *i* or *e* – *giardino*, *gelati*; otherwise hard (as in "gas") – *gatto*. Words ending in *o* are almost always masculine in gender (plural: *-i*); those ending in *a* are generally feminine (plural: *-e*).
- Use the polite second person (*lei*) to speak to strangers, and the informal second person (*tu*) to friends or children.

Courtesies
good morning	buon giorno
good afternoon/ good evening	buona sera
good night	buona notte
hello/goodbye (informal)	ciao
hello (on the telephone)	pronto
goodbye	arrivederci
please	per favore
thank you (very much)	grazie (mille)
you're welcome	prego
how are you? (polite/informal)	come sta/stai?
I'm fine	sto bene
I'm sorry	mi dispiace
excuse me/ I beg your pardon	mi scusi
excuse me (in a crowd)	permesso

Basic vocabulary
yes/no	sì/no
I do not understand	non ho capito
left/right	sinistra/destra
entrance/exit	entrata/uscita
open/closed	aperto/chiuso
good/bad	buono/cattivo
big/small	grande/piccolo
with/without	con/senza
more/less	più/meno
near/far	vicino/lontano
hot/cold	caldo/freddo
early/late	presto/ritardo
here/there	qui/là
now/later	adesso/più tardi
today/tomorrow	oggi/domani
how much is it?	quant'è?
when?/do you have?	quando?/avete?

Emergencies
help!	aiuto!
where is the nearest telephone?	dov'è il telefono più vicino?
there has been an accident	c'è stato un incidente
call the police	chiamate la polizia
call a doctor/ an ambulance	chiamate un medico/ un'ambulanza
first aid	pronto soccorso
where is the nearest hospital?	dov'è l'ospedale più vicino?

INDEX

Citypack
Rome

Important note

Time inevitably brings changes, so always confirm prices, travel facts, and other perishable information when it matters. Although Fodor's cannot accept responsibility for errors, you can use this guide in the confidence that we have taken every care to ensure its accuracy.

Published in the United States by Fodor's Travel Publications, Inc.
Published in the United Kingdom by AA Publishing

Fodor's is a registered trademark of Random House, Inc.

ISBN 0–679–00445–9
Third Edition

FODOR'S CITYPACK ROME

AUTHOR *Tim Jepson*
THIRD EDITION UPDATED BY *Tim Jepson*
CARTOGRAPHY *The Automobile Association*
RV Reise- und Verkehrsverlag
COVER DESIGN *Tigist Getachew, Fabrizio La Rocca*

Acknowledgments

The Automobile Association would like to thank the following photographers, libraries and associations for their assistance in the preparation of this book: © NIPPON TELEVISION NETWORK CORPORATION TOKYO 1991 1; SPECTRUM COLOUR LIBRARY 33b. The remaining pictures are held in the Association's own library (AA PHOTO LIBRARY) with contributions from: M. ADLEMAN 87a; J. HOLMES 5a, 7, 17, 18, 19, 24a, 25, 26, 29a, 29b, 32, 33a, 37a, 38a, 39, 41b, 44, 46a, 46b, 48b, 54, 55, 57, 60; D. MITIDIERI 5b, 12, 13a, 16, 23, 28, 31, 34a, 34b, 35, 38b, 43, 45a, 47, 49a, 49b, 50, 53, 58, 59a, 59b; C. SAWYER 2, 6, 20, 27a, 27b, 30a, 40, 41a; A. SOUTER 13b, 21; P. WILSON 9, 24b, 30b, 36, 37b, 42a, 42b, 45b, 48a, 51, 52, 56, 61, 87b.

Special sales

Fodor's Travel Publications are available at special discounts for bulk purchases (100 copies or more) for sales promotions or premiums. Special editions, including personalized covers, excerpts of existing guides, and corporate imprints, can be created in large quantities for special needs. For more information, contact your local bookseller or write to Special Markets, Fodor's Travel Publications, 201 East 50th Street, New York, NY 10022. Inquiries from Canada should be directed to your local Canadian bookseller or sent to Random House of Canada, Ltd., Marketing Department, 2775 Matheson Blvd. East, Mississauga, Ontario L4W 4P7.

Color separation by Daylight Colour Art Pte Ltd, Singapore
Manufactured by Dai Nippon Printing Co. (Hong Kong) Ltd
10 9 8 7 6 5 4 3 2 1

Titles in the Citypack series

- Amsterdam • Atlanta • Beijing • Berlin • Boston • Chicago • Dublin •
- Florence • Hong Kong • London • Los Angeles • Miami • Montreal •
- New York • Paris • Prague • Rome • San Francisco • Seattle • Shanghai •
- Sydney • Tokyo • Toronto • Venice • Washington, D.C. •

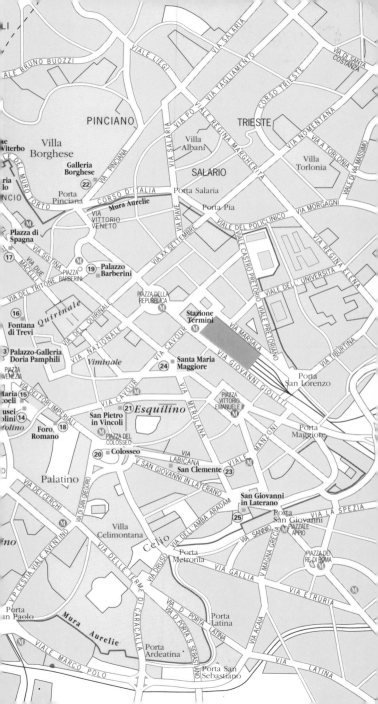

CITYPACK
Rome

The Citypack map covers the city in detail, while the Citypack guide gives you just the information you need to experience the best of Rome:

- The city's top attractions and their must-see sights
- Walks and excursions
- The best museums, churches, parks, fountains, Roman sites, freebies, and more
- Offbeat sights even locals don't know

- Restaurants, hotels, shopping, nightlife— an unabashedly opinionated selection, with pithy descriptions of each recommendation
- Best festivals and events
- Tips on getting the most from your visit

The author: Tim Jepson has written or contributed to many books on Italy. For several years he lived in Italy, during which time he was Rome correspondent for the Sunday Telegraph of London.